THINGS YOU SHOULD KNOW BY NOW

[RELEVANTBOOKS]
WWW.RELEVANTBOOKS.COM

THINGS YOU SHOULD KNOW BY NOW

A MINI LIFE MANUAL FOR THE QUARTERLY AGED

BY JASON BOYETT

[RELEVANTBOOKS]
WWW.RELEVANTBOOKS.COM

Published by Relevant Books
A division of Relevant Media Group, Inc.

www.relevantbooks.com
www.relevantmediagroup.com

© 2003 by Relevant Media Group, Inc.

Cover Design: Raul Justiniano
Interior Design: Danny Jones, Aaron Martin
Relevant Solutions
www.relevant-solutions.com

For information:
RELEVANT MEDIA GROUP, INC.
POST OFFICE BOX 951127
LAKE MARY, FL 32795
407-333-7152

Library of Congress Control Number: 2003090303
International Standard Book Number: 0-9714576-8-9

03 04 05 06 9 8 7 6 5 4 3 2 1

Printed in the United States of America

CONTENTS

ACKNOWLEDGEMENTS

Sincere thanks to: Mike and JoDeane Boyett, my parents, who always told me I should be a writer. Dick and Beverly Storseth, my wife's parents, who consistently prove that in-laws aren't worthy of the bad reputation. My brother, Brooks, a good magician whose insights were vital to the card trick chapter (even though I didn't use his recommended trick). My sister, Micha, a poet whose gift for phrasing and knack for identifying cheese helped shape the final chapter, and who thinks I'm funny even when no one else does. My brother-in-law, Brett Storseth, for his knowledge of pop culture, his proofing expertise and his tactful suggestions on what should be tossed.

My friends and mentors Rod Schroder, Chuck Short, Harrell Stevens, Michael Trimble and Father Robert Busch, who — along with my parents and grandparents—have taught me many of the things I know by now. Katie Meier, my e-mail friend and an excellent writer whose insights on the financial section make me sound a whole lot more knowledgeable than I really am. Cameron Strang and Cara Baker, for the editorial support, the encouragement, and the opportunity.

And most importantly, to Aimee, Ellie, and Owen, who make coming home from work the most enjoyable part of my day.

INTRODUCTION

There's an ancient Zen parable that I've come across in a number of different places. It's a popular story; no doubt you've been introduced to it at some point in your life, whether in a college class, a self-help book, or a professional seminar. The story's everywhere, but that's because it's a good one. Here's how it goes:

A monk is walking through the wilderness one day when he stumbles upon a vicious tiger. Oops. He turns and runs away as fast as he can. The tiger follows. It soon begins gaining on the monk, who is running out of space—a cliff looms ahead. Things don't look good. Suddenly, the man spots a vine anchored to a tree trunk and descending over the edge of the cliff. In a last-ditch effort to save his life, he leaps off the dangerous precipice, grabbing the vine as he falls.

Momentarily safe, the monk looks down. He's suspended over a mass of jagged rocks far below. Letting go would mean certain death. Above him, the tiger paces back and forth, eyeing his next meal. He's running out of options.

Then, of course, it gets worse. At the top of the cliff, two tiny mice skitter out of a hole and begin to gnaw on the vine. Panicking, the monk starts looking around for something to grab onto once worse comes to worse. He searches and searches and suddenly notices a plump wild strawberry growing out of the side of the cliff, barely within reach. He reaches for the strawberry, plucks it and eats it.

"Yum!" the monk says. "That's the most delicious strawberry I've ever had."

The end.[1]

---

[1] Based on the version of the parable as it is told in Paul Reps' and Nyogen Senzaki's *Zen Flesh, Zen Bones: A Collection of Zen and Pre-Zen Writings* (Boston: Tuttle, 1998), 38.

The parable is usually taken for some kind of carpe diem/live-in-the-moment life lesson, because, obviously, the man's plight was not so great he couldn't enjoy a tasty snack, right? Had he worried too much about the past (the tiger) or the future (the rocks), he would have missed out on the present joys of the strawberry.[2]

I'm not so interested in the seize-the-Zen aspects of the above story. Instead, I prefer to look at it as a generational allegory of that no-man's land between college and career—the mid-twenties. We're between identities, between lifestyles, between the tiger of university existence and the jagged rocks of real life. In a book published two years ago, authors Alexandra Robbins and Abby Wilner gave this experience a name: the "quarterlife crisis."[3] They define it as the period between adolescent angst and the responsibilities of established adulthood. With a pat on the back, you're let loose from college, kicked out of your parents' house, and expected to get a real job. And during this transitional stage, you're asked to make countless choices, each of them vital to your well-being. Career. Finances. Relationships. Responsibilities.

It's not easy. Particularly when the mice show up. (Trust me, you'll know them when you see them.)

That's what this book is for. Consider it a miniature and highly selective road map intended to entertain, advise, and guide you from point A (young adulthood) to point B (regular adulthood). In the following pages you'll be introduced to a few things you should know by now, whether "now" for you is post-college, your mid-twenties, or the cusp of thirty. Some of these topics will help you get started on the right foot financially. Others may steer you professionally or socially. Some will save you time or protect you from embarrassment, maybe even heartbreak. And with practice, a handful will make you cooler than everyone else in the room.

---

[2] What you may not have heard is the rest of the story. As the legend goes, D.T. Suzuki, the famed Buddhist scholar and philosopher of religion (and who is generally credited with introducing Zen to America), changed the parable for his listeners stateside. Apparently he thought the real ending wouldn't go over so well with a Western audience, because in the original version, the strawberry turns out to be deadly poison. The monk dies anyway. *Carpe diem*, my friends.

[3] Alexandra Robbins and Abby Wilner, *The Quarterlife Crisis* (New York: J.P. Tarcher, 2001).

A few instructions as you continue. First, don't feel like you have to read this thing front to back, one chapter after another. Consider it fully browsable, formatted for quick, topical digestion.[4] Second, be advised that, in many cases, I'm trying to reduce the varied subject matter to the fewest possible steps or descriptions. My aim is to simplify, because while these are things you ought to know by now, a lot of us don't. Whether explaining why credit card debt is bad or outlining the basic rules of poker, some of the points will be painfully obvious. Eventually you'll be confronted by something you consider common knowledge, and will likely think to yourself: Duh, genius. To which I'll reply: Shut up, Steve. Unless your name isn't Steve, in which case I'll feel pretty foolish.

Anyway, within these pages are a handful of strawberries to down while you're dangling over the cliff. I can't promise that each of them will be the yummiest you've ever had, but more than a few will be quite tasty. All are nutritious, and I'm fairly certain none are poisonous.

At least I hope not.

Thanks for reading, and welcome to quarterlife.

---

[4] And don't forget to read the footnotes.

1

HARD, FIRST DATES ARE EXCEPT ON TV

In *Before Sunrise*, Richard Linklater's talkative mid-nineties date movie starring Ethan Hawke and French actress Julie Delpy, the two main characters have the best date ever. They meet on a train to Vienna, he a wandering American with a Eurail pass, she a French student at the Sorbonne. They're both young, and care-free, and lovers of coffee and conversation. So naturally, they hook up. Their characters, Jessie and Celine, get off the train together to spend a fabulously romantic fourteen hours on the streets of Vienna, talking about everything from music to old flames to the ratios of reincarnation. They fall in love amid witty banter. They meet a street poet. They get their palms read. They kiss. Then Jessie catches a flight back to the States.

I remember reading a review of this movie by Roger Ebert follow-ing its initial release. In it, the revered critic made a statement that seemed so strange I still remember it years later: "This sort of sce-nario has happened, I imagine, millions of times."[1]

Um ... okay. Students, please raise your hand if this has happened to you, or anyone you know, millions of times. Anyone? No? Well, how about at least once? (Thank you, Mr. Ebert. Put your hand down.)

Point is, the up-all-night-intimate-connection-on-the-streets-of-some-twinkly-European-city kind of love affair pretty much hap-pens only in the movies, or on television (Exhibit B: In a late-nineties episode of *Friends*, Ross agrees to take Emily the visiting

---

[1] Roger Ebert, "Review: Before Sunrise," originally published in *Chicago Sun-Times*, January 7, 1995
(*www.suntimes.com/ebert/ebert_reviews/1995/01/962774.html*).

Brit to the opera. By the next morning, they're at a bed-and-break-fast in Vermont. It's all very magical, and they've fallen in love. She ends up being a shrew, by the way.)

Perhaps I've led a sheltered life. Maybe it's because I've never been to Vienna, or because I'm balding prematurely. There's also the fact that I've never locked eyes on a train with a stranger who looked like Julie Delpy. (And it could be, of course, because I'm married.) Whatever the reason, I've never had one of those spon-taneously enchanted dates about which films and TV episodes are made.

Nor, I imagine, have you—even though there never seems to be a lack of these kinds of dating stories on the big and small screen. Why? I think it's because we're not as interested in the real-live dating process as we are the fantasy of it. We dream about meet-ing that perfect someone, of the electric shiver when our hands accidentally touch, or the flicker of interest we hope we just saw in an eyelash flutter or a half-smile across the room. We want movie love, TV romance.

Why else would we watch the voyeuristic date-focused program-ming that has flooded the television airwaves over the last few years? *The Bachelor, The Bachelorette, Blind Date, Chains of Love, Change of Heart, Dismissed, ElimiDATE, The 5th Wheel, Love Cruise, Meet My Folks, Rendez-view*. All of these, at some point or another, found a willing audience. A few are still around. Others have, thank Cupid, dropped into oblivion. But that so many of them appeared within two or three years of each other at the beginning of this century tells us something—we wanted it. We're eager for the contrived mating dance of wine and roses and can-dles and, well, camera crews. We eat that kind of stuff up. Then we go out on a real-life blind date with Stacy, cousin of Lydia from work. Unfortunately, Stacy hates dogs and you have a dog and she's vegetarian and you took her to a steakhouse and she's got this piece of lettuce plastered against one of her teeth the entire meal and, sorry, it just doesn't work out. Date's over. You go home alone.

Where's the pre-dawn kiss on the streets of Vienna? Where's the Vermont bed-and-breakfast? Where are the street poets?

Answer: They're on TV. But in real-world dating experienced by living, breathing, three-dimensional people—people like you and me—these kinds of things don't happen. As my wife, not one to mince words, once said after watching an episode of one of those dating reality shows, "These people are so stupid. This gives people a stupid idea of what dating is."

So here's something you should know by now: Dating on TV is stupid. It's not how it works in real life. First dates are never as easy as they appear in the movies (for instance, don't expect every date—let alone a first date—to, ahem, "invite you up for coffee" at the end of the evening). Nor are they as expensive as the television often makes it out to be. Or as complicated. (Ever been in one of those situations where you mistakenly book two dates for one evening? Ever thought you could actually pull it off? No? Well it happens all the time on TV, to everyone from Fonzie to Felicity.)

By putting too much stock into what, for simplicity's sake, we'll call "TV Dating," you're getting a distorted idea of the process. You'll end up with the aforementioned "stupid idea of what dating is." For your benefit, I've identified the following first date media archetypes to delete from your brain:

1) THE DATE OF GREAT EXPENSE

Back to *Friends*. Courteney Cox's Monica meets Pete, a seemingly regular guy played by Jon Favreau, at the diner where she's temporarily working. He butters on the charm, convincing her to go out for dinner with him. "I know this great Italian place," Pete explains. Monica consents. So our man Pete—who turns out to be an Internet billionaire—flies her to Italy. For dinner. First date. Someone she'd never met before in her life. Happens all the time to people like Roger Ebert.

Related to the above scenario, but to a less preposterous degree, is the pricey night-on-the-town date. Since a vast amount of television shows are set in New York City, let's use that environment as an example. How many dates on TV involve some combination of the following? Dinner at the Four Seasons or its equivalent in midtown Manhattan (for two, expect to cough up $150 for drinks, a meal, taxes, and tips). Following the meal is some swanky event.

Perhaps a charity ball? That's another $150 a head. Knicks tickets? Expect upwards of fifty dollars a seat. Add a cab to the mix, and you're out at least three hundred bucks for the date.

Now let's be honest here. Short of the night you propose marriage, is it necessary to spend that much on a date? More importantly, will you ever have the cash flow to even consider it? Most people my age don't. And if you're expecting some guy (or girl) to come around flashing enough currency to do the above, well, stop. Stop with the outsized expectations—it won't happen that often. If you do encounter it, proceed cautiously. What's he trying to prove? What does he hope to gain? Is he generous or just showing off? Is the guy trying to snow you on the first date by spending fist loads of money? Does he want you to be impressed by him or his income?

All the above are questions worth asking, but here's something about which there's no question at all: If a guy wants to take you to dinner in Rome and you live in Akron, he's trying too hard. Way too hard. Score one for overcompensation.

2) THE HIGHLY INAPPROPRIATE VENUE

In *Singles*, Cameron Crowe's 1992 ode to Seattle, Campbell Scott and Kyra Sedgwick first meet each other at a concert. It's a memorable scene. Standing fifteen feet from a prototypical grunge band stomping around on stage, the two singles attempt the awkward, "Hi, come here often?" introductory conversation. That's difficult enough as it is, but even worse when standing shoulder-to-shoulder in a head-nodding sea of near-moshers, shouting at each other above the power chords and budding tinnitus.[2] The two eventually get together, then break up, then get together again—but nothing really happens in the first place until they meet each other again in a quieter, more intimate setting.

So ... live music venues—not a good place for a first date. Same goes for a dance club, unless the two of you have both acknowledged a fondness for the activity. Don't expect much in the way of conversation, though. Also movies. Consider *Seinfeld*. Remember

---

[2] tin·ni·tus (noun): a ringing or buzzing in the ears. In *Singles*, Campbell Scott refers to it as "club disease." Just so you'll know.

when Jerry's date "shushed" him and Elaine during a visit to the Cineplex? Jerry got all huffy about it and broke up with her. But I sided with the date. I supported the "shush." When I go to a movie (or a concert, for that matter), I intend to pay attention. Two-and-a-half hours in a dark room with booming audio is not the best occasion to get to know another person. So why select it for a first date?

3) THE QUEST FOR SEX

Here's where it gets fun. I refer you to the generally sleazy world of TV dating shows, the plots for which can be summed up as "skeezy twentysomethings trying to get laid." I reference the syndicated *Blind Date*, MTV's *Dismissed*, and *ElimiDATE*, a *Survivor*-esque competition show. For instance, here's an episode summary taken from BlindDateTV.com, the website for the show of the same name. The summary is typical, as is the bad spelling, awkward sentence construction, and ridiculous grammar:

> Kara is the manger (sic) of a software company that (sic) hates fake people. Her claim to fame is she loves to get people naked. Keith is a martial arts champ that (sic, blah blah blah) likes his freedom and loves to have fun. The two begin their day at a water park where Keith asks if she finds him sexy. Next, the two go to a Nature Preserve where Keith makes sexual innuendoes about a shark they see. Over dinner Kara promises to kiss Keith once they get on the boat. It's there where Kara convinces her date to take it all off and jump into the ocean. Find out what happens after his skinny dipping experience![3]

You'll also encounter a lot of body shots, public hot tubbing, skimpy bathing suits, skimpy bathing suits being removed ... you get the picture. Remember, kids, these are blind dates—people who didn't know each other prior to the show (which doesn't stop

---

[3] Episode summary, *www.blinddatetv.com*. I ran across this summary while browsing the official site in August of 2002. Unfortunately, I didn't record the airdate of the Kara/Keith episode, nor have I been able to locate this summary since. I haven't seen the real episode either, so you're just gonna have to trust me on this.

them from, say, licking ice cream off each other's abdomens within an hour). Point is: not your typical date.

I'll defer again to my wife, who excels in commentary about these kinds of shows. "The women are all surgically-enhanced and desperate," she says. "The guys are all horndogs. The feeling you get from it is that all the girls are thinking, 'If I act like a whore, he'll like me.' And the guys are thinking, 'She's acting like a whore. I like her.' Then they get drunk."

Keep in mind that all this is captured by, and willfully released to, cameramen and a national audience. I don't think I have to do much explaining here—this isn't the best picture of dating. Don't expect body shots and public nudity on your first date. Don't expect to be followed around by a camera crew, either.

So don't follow the bad examples of the entertainment world when contemplating a first date with someone. Don't make it too expensive, don't choose the wrong venue, and don't look forward to it ending up in the sack. Don't count on anything being easy.

Enough with the negatives. How can you make a first date successful? Be friendly and courteous. Be on time. Choose the right activity (one that lets you get to know one another and is something you enjoy). Go someplace affordable. Keep it relatively short. Plan on talking about yourself, but be prepared to ask a lot of questions about your date. Make eye contact. Find common ground. Be curious, warm, and enthusiastic. Ask non-threatening, open-ended questions. Keep the focus on the present rather than the past (old flames) or future (a potential relationship). Pay attention. Be real.

If none of those work, you're going to have to fire up the jet and head for Rome.

WHAT MARRIAGE ISN'T

2

An interesting thing happened in the spring of 2002. Marriage, long subject to rumors of its impending demise, suddenly became cool. In March, MTV premiered *The Osbournes*, its outrageously popular reality series in which we watched the previously unexemplary-in-every-way Ozzy share heartfelt kisses with his doting wife, Sharon. Between fits of sarcasm and F-bomb detonations, the network's rabid audience was treated to weekly displays of the Osbournes' obvious love for each other. No less than Dan Quayle embraced them as good examples for the rest of us.

In April, two best-selling books fought for shelf space at Barnes and Noble. *Married: A Fine Predicament*, written by Anne Roiphe, a liberal feminist and insightful essayist, recommended marriage as something that, ultimately, leads to joy and fulfillment. From the opposite spectrum, conservative criminologist James Q. Wilson discussed *The Marriage Problem: How Our Culture Has Weakened Families*, in which he attributed a variety of societal dilemmas to the devaluing of the institution. Both took different paths, but reached the same conclusion: Marriage is good for you.

In May, a multicultural group called the Alliance for Marriage introduced the proposed (and controversial) Federal Marriage Amendment to Congress, with bi-partisan support. Its stated purpose? "To call upon leaders of Congress to defend both marriage and democracy in America by introducing a constitutional amendment designed to preserve the legal status of marriage for future generations." [1]

---

[1] The full text of the amendment can be read at the Alliance for Marriage website, located at *www.allianceformarriage.org*.

A few weeks later, actress Candace Bergen—she of the great Murphy Brown versus Dan Quayle debate in the early nineties regarding the importance of fathers in child-raising—told the Associated Press that she sided with the former Veep. "His speech was a perfectly intelligent speech about fathers not being dispensable," she admitted, "and nobody agreed with that more than I did."[2]

Touchdown, marriage.

So, with everyone else jumping on the marriage train, should you go ahead and buy your ticket? As someone who's been happily married since my junior year of college, I can answer that without so much as a flinch: yes. I recommend it. It's fun. It's fulfilling. It keeps you warm at night.

Of course, so does a puppy, which is considerably cheaper than a wedding ceremony and much less slobbery. That leads us to the crux of the matter. Marriage is a wonderful institution, but it's not always the best choice for everybody.

Marriage is like a tube of toothpaste: You get the best results when you start squeezing at the bottom. (Insert your own marital hanky-panky joke here.) The most successful marriages start with a solid foundation. That foundation is built on many things—mutual interests, shared beliefs, selflessness, and, of course, love—but the biggest problem going into many marriages is that those basics are often held back by unrealistic expectations.

All of us know someone for whom the first marriage didn't work out. We've all heard the statistics. First marriages have a failure rate of more than 40 percent.[3] Second marriages end in divorce 60

---

[2] Bergen: "Dan Quayle Was Right About Murphy," FOXNEWS.com (posted July 11, 2002, at *www.foxnews.com/story/0,2933,57440,00.html*).

[3] The commonly cited statistic is that 50 percent of marriages end in divorce. This number is usually arrived at by comparing the number of marriages and divorces in a given year—which usually occur at a two to once clip, thus the conclusion of a 50 percent divorce rate. However, that fails to consider marriages in total (especially people who are already married, and have been for a long time). A better statistic is this: Of first marriages, 43 percent end in separation or divorce within fifteen years. Source: Matthew Bramlett and William Mosher. "First marriage dissolution, divorce, and remarriage: United States," *Advance Data From Vital and Health Statistics*: No.323 (Hyattsville, MD: National Center for Health Statistics) 21.

percent of the time. This is particularly true of the generation whose parents married (and subsequently divorced) in the 1970s. For them marriage seems to have become something like the process of selecting a dog from the pound. You look around until one catches your eye and convinces you to take him home. He's all tail-wagging and kisses at first. Then, gradually, he proceeds to chew up your Timberlands and pee on your couch and leave hair all over your pillow. So you take him back. You tell the folks at the pound that he didn't work out. You move on.[4]

Marriages can end up the same way because of our misplaced expectations. We think we know what marriage is because we've seen it on TV. It's Monica and Chandler, all candles and sex and witty banter. It's the end-of-the-day slow dancing of Cliff and Claire Huxtable. It's the tuxedos and pigtailed flower girls and white chiffon spectacle of *A Wedding Story* on TLC. Then, when everything doesn't turn out exactly as we dreamed, we look for an out, blame it on irreconcilable differences, and scrap the covenant.

The differences aren't the problem, though; our irreconcilable expectations are. Let's look, then, at some of those predetermined ideas and dump marriage out of its box. Here's something you should know by now: not what marriage is, but what it isn't.

A CURE FOR LONELINESS

In a society where we're plugged in twenty-four hours a day, where "community" is more often used to describe a chat room than an actual neighborhood, people long to connect intimately with someone. Ours is a society that puts great emphasis on "hooking up." Being alone is hard.

We see couples everywhere—in restaurants, on TV, on the bus or train or sidewalks on the way to work—and feel like something is missing in our lives if we're alone. As humans, we have an innate

---

[4] I recommend *The Starter Marriage and the Future of Matrimony*, by Pamela Paul (New York: Random House, 2002). In it, Paul—an editor for *American Demographics*—examines the growing phenomenon of twentysomethings who are getting married and divorcing within a few years, before kids arrive. She calls this low-commitment first union a "starter marriage," and discusses its impact upon Generation X.

need to belong, and we expect a spouse to provide that sense of acceptance and intimacy and comfort. We're Jerry Maguire looking for a soul mate, someone to whom we can say, "You complete me."

Best case scenario, that's what a good marriage will provide. But I know couples in loving relationships who remain lonely. Why? After all, they've found a perfect mate who has taken great strides toward fulfilling their need for intimacy. But that's a heavy load for one person to bear, despite the stories Cameron Crowe tells. Lonely single people become lonely married people. If your goal in marriage is to satisfy your need to belong, your next stop may be heartbreak.

AN ESCAPE FROM BOREDOM

In 1991, *U.S. News and World Report* reported that half of U.S. workers said the reason they have a job—aside from needing to earn a living—was to keep from being bored. In a separate survey, 25 percent of teenagers said they drink alcohol for the same reason.[5] Drug abuse experts almost always cite boredom as a leading excuse for experimenting with drugs. That's where all the talk about idle minds and the devil's workshop comes from—we do stuff simply because there's nothing else to do.

What does this have to do with marriage? Plenty. Some couples get married to shake off boredom. Life becomes dull, and it's easy to convince yourself that a serious relationship will make the day more bearable. It's something else to do, the next step after graduating college and getting a job and exploring the dating scene. When you get married, you expect built-in happiness. Automatic entertainment. Regular conversation. At least you'll have someone to watch TV with.

Unfortunately, this fails to account for the true cause of boredom, which isn't necessarily an external lack of stimulus, but rather an internal one. You're not bored because you've seen every episode of *The Real World: New Orleans* thirty times. You're bored because you can't come up with something better to do after watching it the first time. It's not my fault you're bored, nor is it MTV's fault. It's yours.

---

[5] *U. S. News and World Report* (June 24, 1991), 14.

Getting married in order to generate a little excitement in your life is a terrible motivation. Why? Because once the merry-go-round stops—once the novelty wears out—you'll immediately start looking for the next ride.

A ROWDY SEX ROMP

As the old experiment goes, put a penny in a jar for every time you have sex during the first year of marriage. Then, beginning at the start of your second year, take a penny out every time you do the horizontal two-step. Chances are, a couple of years later, you'll still be pulling pennies.

Does the sex stop after twelve months of good lovin'? No. Not by any means. But is every night a page out of the *Karma Sutra*? Nope. Despite what guys think, your wife won't always want to wear that see-through teddy. Elastic and lace just aren't that comfortable in some places. And ladies? Keeping the romance alive is hard work for us guys. Sometimes we just want to watch *SportsCenter*.

Still, with communication and sensitivity, sex can (and should) remain a vital part of marriage. It's the ultimate bonding activity for a couple to share. But remember it's not the only activity. Don't expect marriage to be a fifty-year honeymoon of libido and lipstick.

A MEANS TO A MAKEOVER

How many times have you heard this? "He's not really interested in the stuff I like to do, but that'll change once we get married." Very few marriages that launch from that pad end up happily ever after.

If there's anything you should know about marriage, it's this: saying "I do" may change your legal relationship, but it doesn't change your character. An unhappy single person will be an unhappy married person. A thoughtless single person will be a thoughtless married person. An annoying single person will be an annoying married person. The point is, don't enter a marriage expecting to remake your husband or wife into someone else. You can't. People have baggage, stuff they've wheeled around behind

11

them since high school. It's been with us so long, very few have the willpower to drop it before entering the wedding chapel. The flaws go with you—right down the aisle, up the steps, on the honeymoon, and over the threshold.

Don't marry someone for who they might become. Marry them for who they are right now. Otherwise, they're likely to become nothing more than your ex.

AN EASY TRANSITION

There's a reason romantic movies end, rather than begin, with a wedding. It's because that's when the hard stuff starts. You have to take down the decorations and pick the rose petals up off the yard. You have to unpack after the honeymoon and write insincere thank-you notes for the tacky bathmats. You have to get used to sharing a closet and a bed and a refrigerator and a sink with another person. For anyone who's lived on their own for any length of time, the space between singleness and marriage is a wide one. It's a difficult transition for many.

"I wasn't ready for all the changes," a friend of mine once told me about his first few months of marriage. "I could deal with moving into her place and giving up my furniture—it was pretty much crap anyway. But what surprised me was having to deal with her emotions. When you're dating, you always see her best face. Once you get married, you see everything."

Women don't have it any easier. Many secretly wince at the notion of placing their fate alongside that of another, worrying that the role of wife might eat into their sense of individuality. Toss in holidays spent with another family and comparisons with Mom's cooking, and you've got some explosive issues to deal with from the onset.

There's no way around making these adjustments. In order for the marriage to last more than a week or two, you'll have to find a way to cope. Don't be taken by surprise; expect a few hiccups going in.

Sheesh. When my wife reads this, I'm going to have to do some explaining. (Aimee: "What are you trying to say? That I'm boring?

That I need to change? That we don't have enough sex?" Jason: "You're pretty.")

Let me get a head start by ending with this disclaimer. We've been discussing what marriage is not, but here's what marriage is: Marriage is wonderful. There is no better way to make it through life than with a partner who loves you despite your morning breath, despite your stinky Converse All-Stars, and despite your failure to clean coffee stains. Marriage is deeply satisfying, incredibly fulfilling, and loads of fun. It makes the harsh edges of life a little softer. It brings joy and hope and laughter. And as I said before, I highly recommend it.

But it's not easy, and it's not something to rush into without thinking. When nearly half of all Gen-X marriages are ending in divorce, it tells me that a lot of us are taking the plunge without knowing what's in the pool. Expectations aren't being met, and folks are climbing out hurt and disappointed.

Don't let that happen to you. Know the benefits. Know the challenges. Know your potential mate. Get your expectations right. Then, jump in with both feet. You're gonna like it.

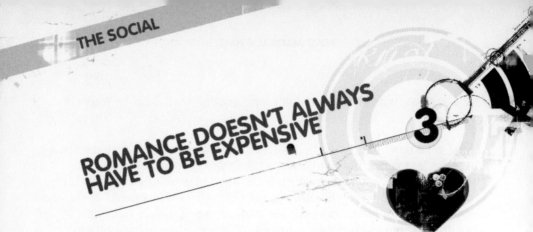

ROMANCE DOESN'T ALWAYS HAVE TO BE EXPENSIVE

3

In any dating, engaged, or married relationship, it's important to maintain the thing that brought the couple together in the first place: romance. Without romance, a marriage can be little more than an economic and social partnership, a mutually beneficial lifestyle choice. It's like using a television set to fill the rectangular void in your entertainment center, but never actually turning the set on—everything looks and feels right, but the object itself is being wasted. It's not living up to its potential.

Or to use another dorky metaphor, romance is the water that causes the seed of a relationship to grow. Problem is, we're all going thirsty because we're intimidated by the watering process. Romance looks too hard. It seems too expensive. The plants on TV are being watered from a crystal decanter, and all we've got is an empty Coke can.

For some reason, our culture has come to equate romance with money. I'm no expert, but I can identify a few culprits.

Most elaborate and expensive movie ever made: *Titanic*, at a cost of an estimated $200 million, and the most successful film ever. For those who haven't seen it (both of you, listen up), it was a historical romance between the lovely Kate Winslett and a kid named Leo. I forget what he looks like. Did I mention it was a romance?

Most memorable and expensive day of your life: your wedding. According to *Bride* magazine's "2000 State of the Union" report, it costs an average of $19,000—give or take a bridesmaid—to turn a dream into a real-life wedding ceremony. And that's before the honeymoon.

Most elaborate and expensive mausoleum ever built: the breathtaking Taj Mahal in Agra, India. Finished in 1631, the Taj Mahal is the result of the promise of a powerful and infinitely wealthy king to his dying wife. Mumtaz Mahal, beloved of the reigning Shah Jahan, died giving birth to their fourteenth child. According to legend, she spent her last moments extracting from her husband a pledge to honor their great love by constructing a burial chamber more beautiful than any the world had seen. Jahan performed admirably, commissioning a delicately ethereal—some say near perfect—structure of uncommon harmony, grace, and wealth. Jahan was obsessed with architectural flawlessness and artistry; he hauled in white marble, red sandstone, and vast amounts of precious stones from all corners of his empire, embellishing the walls of the mausoleum with pearls, diamonds, emeralds, and sapphires. Consider it bling, 17th century style.[1]

So there you have it: The most romantic movie, the most romantic day, the most romantic gift, all three of which are/were extravagantly expensive. Romance is a wallet-drainer, right? You want to show a girl you love her? Impress a guy? Then toss around some cash, go to an expensive restaurant, build a jewel-encrusted wonder of the modern world to his memory. Rent a limo, a horse-drawn carriage, a cabin in Veil, and she'll love you forever.

At least that's what it seems like in today's money-conscious society. I blame it on our inclination to take our cues on how the world works from the media. Here's a test: Think of a romantic dinner. Picture it in your mind. Most likely, your vision involves a white linen tablecloth, silver serving platters, and crystal stemware in an intimate, hushed atmosphere. Why? Because the venue for a romantic dinner in movies and television is most often a fancy restaurant. Same goes for romantic gifts (jewelry) and flowers (a dozen red roses). When was the last time a guy showed up for a date with a bouquet of daisies? Or a single white rose?

I once ran across a statistic that we ought to consider at this point. I once stumbled upon one of those ubiquitous romance and dating websites where an author cited a survey in which 80 percent of women said their marriage proposal was less romantic than they'd hoped. That's no surprise—guys can be ridiculously lazy, unimaginative, and heavy-handed when it comes to proposing

---

[1] Taj Mahal: Memorial to Love," PBS.org: *Treasures of the World* (Posted 1999 at *www.pbs.org/treasuresoftheworld/a_nav/taj_nav/main_tajfrm.html*

marriage (billboard on I-40, anyone?). More remarkable was a corollary stat attached to the survey. Participants were asked how much their fiancé had spent on the proposal. Most popular answer? At least three hundred dollars.[2]

The moral of the story: Limousines, fancy restaurants, and a Lear jet to Paris are no guarantees of romance. In fact, the most romantic gestures are more likely to be inexpensive. Why? Because they are personal. They are creative. They may take time and effort, but they aren't mass-produced. They aren't for sale somewhere, and that's what makes them romantic.

So, this is what you should know by now: Romance doesn't always have to be expensive. In fact, the most romantic activities are often the most economical. Here's why.

BEING ROMANTIC IS ABOUT THE SMALL STUFF.

For any romantic relationship to develop and thrive—husband and wife, boyfriend and girlfriend, sci-fi geek and George Lucas—there must be some sort of intimate connection. Intimacy is wrapped up in details: the way she twirls her hair when she's nervous, the way he shivers when you brush your fingers against the back of his neck. That kind of familiarity requires the interplay of thoughts, hopes, dreams, fears—all wrapped up in tiny, fragile moments of transparency with each other.

So why propose marriage on the JumboTron at the next Dodgers game?

As relationships expert Greg Godek once put it, romance is "much more about the small gestures—the little ways of making daily life with your lover a bit more special" than it is about the big, gaudy, extravagant stuff.[3]

---

[2] The author of the website attributed these statistics to a 1998 survey in the *New Orleans Times-Picayune*. I haven't been able to locate the actual survey, so the specific stats may be unreliable. But I don't doubt the accuracy of the results — most women probably are a little disappointed in the popping of the long-awaited question.

[3] Gregory J.P. Godek, *1001 Ways to Be Romantic* (New York: Casablanca Press, 1993), 1.

The small gestures are the things you do that break from the daily routine and let your loved one know that he or she is special. I will occasionally get in my car to go to work in the morning and find that my wife, Aimee, has attached a stickie note to the steering wheel, one that simply tells me that she loves me. Sometimes it's a phone call or an e-mail in the middle of the day, for no reason other than to say, "Hi."

Other examples of "small stuff": holding hands in public; bringing home a favorite flower; making your own bookmark (with a special note) and putting it inside the book she's reading; sitting with him on the couch to watch the game—the whole game; walking in the door with an ice cream treat; arranging to have a note, a flower, or breakfast left on his desk at work; telling her you love her at unexpected or inappropriate times (like during a movie, at the top of the roller coaster, or, ahem, during a sermon).

BEING ROMANTIC IS ABOUT THE UNEXPECTED.

The Western world has a problem. Actually, several problems, but only one of which applies to this essay: the romantic mandate. There are a handful of days on our calendar—days like Valentine's Day, Christmas, or a birthday—at which time those in romantic relationships must meet the societal directive of romanticism. You'd better get your loved one a gift and a card on those days, because if you don't, you're toast. For that reason, Valentine's gifts are usually uninspired boxes of chocolates or bouquets of roses. The card is something you grabbed at Wal-Mart on the way home, body-checking your way through the throng of sweaty, nervous men swarming the American Greetings aisle. The result is hardly special and nothing any different from what every other male in the world is doing. As Godek has written, these are obligatory romance days, events you are required to remember and act upon, but for which you get exactly zero props.[4] None. Roses on February 14? Unoriginal, unimaginative, and downright expensive. Sorry. Doesn't count. Not romantic.

---

[4] Godek, 41.

What's truly romantic is a gift that comes out of nowhere, like a rose a day for the twelve days leading up to Valentine's Day.[5] Or, instead of a fancy Valentine's dinner out (just like everyone else is doing), rent her favorite DVD and garnish it with pizza and a bottle of bubbly. Or, simply, offer a foot rub without being asked.

You see where we're going with this? Whether it's for Valentine's Day, a birthday, or Columbus Day, a gift is romantic not because of the price, but because of the sentiment—the thought and effort put into it. A well-timed greeting card given on an otherwise uneventful day will be treasured more than an expensive birthday gift, for one simple reason: The card is neither compulsory nor expected. No one made you do it.

BEING ROMANTIC IS ABOUT CREATIVITY.

A romantic gesture is cherished when the experience of it is completely unique, when the recipient knows that he or she is the only one opening this gift, reading this card, or enjoying this moment. How do you do it? Simple. Don't settle for the status quo.

Are you the kind of person who buys a nice greeting card, signs your name inside, and stuffs it into the envelope? If so, shame on you. The rules of creative romance dictate that you make greeting cards personal. This means writing a personal note in every card you give—even if it's as simple as "I love you because ..." and then listing one or two good qualities. Simply putting your name on something Hallmark designed and wrote requires no thought or effort whatsoever. You might as well give a card that says, "I'm too lazy for anything else," then signing your name. Mass-production = bad.

Of course, not everyone's a writer, and many are uncomfortable putting thoughts into coherent words ("I might end up accidentally calling her fat," one of my friends lamented about love notes). A solution is to get creative with quantity instead of quality. One year I bought Aimee a box of Scooby-Doo kids' valentines, the

---

[5] Here's a secret: Twelve single, unadorned roses bought separately will end up being less expensive than a dozen roses elaborately arranged into a bouquet. Score one for both creativity *and* frugality.

small ones children give their teachers and friends. I wrote simple little notes in all 30 (i.e., "You're pretty" or "I love you") and left them around the house, in her car, in her purse—all over the place—for her to find throughout the day. Much less expensive than a box of chocolates and far more memorable.

A bouquet of flowers is generally not too creative—but a bouquet of something other than flowers is. For instance, multiples of her favorite candy, or a basket of bathtub stuff (soaps, oils, lotions). And who says guys don't like a bouquet? I'd be perfectly happy to accept, for instance, a collection of socket wrenches. Or Cubs tickets. Or dry flies.[6] Find ways to fit the gift to the recipient, and you're on your way to romance.

Relationships are hard enough without being complicated by the money issue. In a world where going out is activity-oriented, it's hard to date when you're poor. It's harder still to be married on a budget. But simple, thoughtful romance greases the relationship wheel, and though romance can cost a fortune, it certainly doesn't have to. What it does cost, without fail, is a little time and effort. It means going out of the way to bring happiness to the one you love. And if you can't bring yourself to do that, then maybe you should ask yourself this first: Am I really in love?

---

[6] For the uninitiated, a "dry fly" is an artificial insect used by flyfishermen. It's intended to look like a bug drifting on the surface of the water, and is used to tempt and catch fish (mainly trout) via the art of fly fishing. Artifical flies have fun names like Blue Wing Olive and Elk Hair Caddis. You know in *The River Runs Through It* when Brad Pitt was slinging that line so gracefully into the water? At the end of his line was an artificial fly. Of course, it was a wet fly, not a dry one, but let's save that for later.

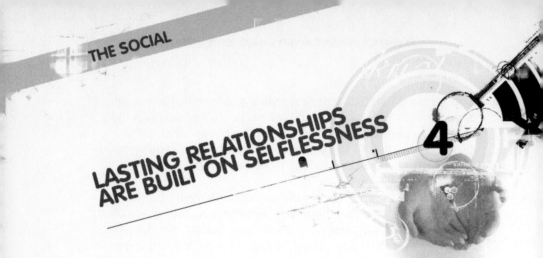

LASTING RELATIONSHIPS ARE BUILT ON SELFLESSNESS

4

There's a folktale told about a peculiar landmark on the outskirts of the bustling port city of Kaohsiung in Southern Taiwan, a mountain called Ban Pin Shan—literally, "half-faced mountain." It resembles the leftover crown of a half-eaten cupcake, bit right through the top. According to legend, here's how it got that way:

Years ago, the mountain was still whole, and a small fishing village lay in its foothills. One day, an elderly stranger entered the village. His long hair and beard were white as clouds, his clothes ragged and torn. He brought with him a crate full of hot dumplings, the delicious aroma of which could be smelled throughout the village. A crowd soon gathered around him.

The man began to shout, "Hot and delicious dumplings!" His voice rose above the curious onlookers. "One for ten cents, two for twenty cents, three for free!"

The crowd murmured. Three for free? No one did business that way. They concluded the old man must be insane, or some sort of trickster. Still, the crowd kept growing and the man kept shouting. "Dumplings! Hot and delicious! One for ten, two for twenty, three for free!"

As the story goes, a villager with the unfortunate name of BigHead Wang was the first to take up the strange old man on his offer. "Who cares if it's a trick?" said Wang. "I'll find out whether they're really free." So Wang stepped up and ordered three steaming dumplings. His face lit up as he popped the first, as big as a chicken's egg, into his mouth. "Yum!" he said. He then ate the second dumpling, but quickly grew so full he could hardly think about eating more.

The old man held out his open palm. "Twenty cents," he said. Wang swallowed. "If I eat three dumplings, I don't have to pay, right?"

The old man assured him that three dumplings were indeed free. So Wang stuffed one last dumpling into his mouth. The stranger kept his word and didn't charge BigHead Wang a cent. The deal was legit. The villagers went crazy; men and women began ordering and eating dumplings as fast as possible. Everyone received three free dumplings—no one ordered just one or two—until finally the crate was empty. The old man smiled and left. Those who hadn't received a dumpling were utterly disappointed.

That evening and the next morning, word began to spread about the crazy dumpling man. "Who is this man?" villagers asked. "Where did he come from? What are his dumplings made of? Why would he give them away?"

On the second day, the peculiar old man returned, with a crate full of fresh dumplings. "Hot and delicious dumplings!" he shouted. "One for ten cents, two for twenty, three for free!" A near riot ensued, and the townspeople began consuming the dumplings so hurriedly that they hardly remembered to chew. The crate emptied within minutes.

The same thing happened again on day three. Villagers pressed against the feeble old man like wolves on a wounded deer, grasping and snapping at each other to edge nearer the prized dumplings, until finally a single voice rose out of the crowd. "Mister?" a young man said. "I'd like only one dumpling. Just one, please."

The frenzy came to a standstill. "Pardon me," said the old man, "but did you hear me clearly? I said one for ten, two for twenty, three for free. Why do you ask for only one?"

The young man fidgeted with his hands. "I feel bad for you," he said. "You've carried this huge load of dumplings to us everyday, and we've enjoyed them so much. But you've not made any money yet. I want to help, so please give me only one dumpling. I'd like to pay." The gluttonous villagers backed away from the old man and his ravaged dumpling crate. They hung their heads in shame.

Suddenly, the old man let out a laugh so loud and clear that the crowd stumbled backwards in fright. "A-ha! At last I have found you!" he shouted. "You, young man, are the only person in this village suitable to be my pupil."

"Dumpling man, who are you?" BigHead Wang asked, licking his sticky fingers.

The old man gave a cryptic grin and pointed. "I am the god from behind that mountain." As the villagers turned their heads, they noticed that half the mountain was missing—a huge chunk was gone, as if it had been cut away by a giant's sword. The horrible truth dawned on them, and the crowd rushed back to the crate. Where the dumplings had been, there was only black, oozing mud. The mountain god had fed them the soil of the mountain itself.

The kind-hearted young man soon departed with the deity to learn the ways of magic. And the villagers wept, sick and disgusted at their selfishness. They named the mountain Ban Pin Shan— "half-faced mountain"—and would forever remember their greed toward the gifts of the mountain god.[1]

My wife and I married young. I was twenty-one, Aimee was twenty—we've been happily married now for eight years. That's twice as long as many of our peers' marriages, so we get asked from time to time to offer a few hints toward sustaining a good marriage. Our answer is the same every time. In fact, we don't even have to confer anymore. What's the secret to a lasting relationship? It's a lack of selfishness, and it applies to both members of the relationship. When a couple sheds selfishness like wedding

---

[1] "Ban Pin Shan," *Folk Stories of Taiwan*; to order write: Houston Taiwanese School of Languages and Culture (HTSLC), 7511 Coachwood Drive, Houston, TX 77071. The legend of Ban Pin Shan can also be viewed at the *Folk Stories of Taiwan* website: *www.taiwandc.org/folk-ban.htm*.

clothes in a honeymoon suite, then refuses to put it back on once the relationship's consummated, that couple is on the road to marital triumph.

That's something you should know by now: Self-sacrifice is the key to any lasting relationship, however it may be classified—married, engaged, dating, platonic, you name it. It's a relatively simple concept, one that basically comes down to just one thing: what you do with the dumplings.

"Finally," you're thinking. "I was wondering how that convoluted story applied to anything." To which I reply, "Settle down, BigHead Wang. It's all just a clever allegory. And an interesting story. And what's a guy named 'BigHead' doing criticizing my chapter introduction anyway?"

I thought so.

Relationships are hard. While this may come as a colossal shock to most of you, take my word for it—sharing your life with another person is no run through a sun-dappled wheat field. What trips us up is that "sharing" part, because when we enter into any relationship, we expect dumplings. The figurative kind. We decide to date someone (or even befriend someone) based on what we might gain from them. But rarely do we give thought to what we might be able to give. We get so excited about the dumplings another person might serve us—love, pleasure, confidence, companionship, comfort, support, sex—that we devour those things at the expense of the other, and to the detriment of the relationship.

Some people are fantastic givers. My wife is an example. She's the one who coordinates meals for new parents in our Sunday school class, who throws baby showers for the less fortunate and the overwhelmed. At six months pregnant and enduring the perpetual small-frame/big-baby discomfort of our second child, she had the audacity to offer me backrubs. She worried about keeping me up at night when she went through a third-trimester phase of sleeplessness—never mind that she needed the rest far more than I. On top of all that, she's a mother already, and all mothers are selfless. It's an instinct, as spontaneous as licking a finger to de-smudge a child's face.

People like Aimee share and share and share, and their dumplings always seem to magically replenish. So their spouses, partners and friends get into the habit of taking and taking and taking. It seems to work fine for a while. The dumplings are yummy, and they show up again the next day. But what happens when, one morning, the dumplings are gone? What happens when the dust clears and you're left with a crumbling mountain in the distance, a half-faced relationship? What happens when we realize what our heedless appetite has destroyed?

Those questions are gristle to a healthy relationship, because by nature, we're selfish people. It's part of the survival/self-preservation package that we're born with. Still, each of us has the capacity for thoughtfulness, community, and generosity hidden somewhere beneath our me-first predisposition. Many of us didn't know it—nor did we expect it—but those qualities boiled to the surface in September of 2001. Earlier that year, before the economic bubble had burst, we'd been gobbling up personal gain like candy (or, since we're on the subject, dumplings), stuffing our faces full of stock options, self-help theories, "revolutionary" diet plans, and four-dollar caffeine boosts. We were self-made, focused, worldly, and independent. Despite the lofty role it plays in our religious and moral codes, self-sacrifice was dead last on our daily to-do lists. If it showed up at all.

Then came September 11, 2001, and out of the tragedy and rubble and terror rose a surprising phoenix—a sincere (if short-lived) return to national selflessness. For the next several days, we focused less on work and more on our relationships and families. We stood in line for hours to give blood. We gathered food and medical supplies, we gave money, we waved flags. We cheered our firefighters, policemen, and emergency workers. And that wasn't all. According to the *Houston Chronicle*, an even more peculiar turnaround occurred. Divorce dismissals in Harris County—Houston, Texas—spiked to three times normal levels in the two weeks following September 11. That's divorce dismissals. Couples used the tragedy as a springboard to self-sacrifice within their failing marriages. They suddenly became more willing to patch things up.[2] Another report indicated that engaged couples began spending far less time worrying about wedding plans—the

---

[2] Mary Flood, "Couples Want Peace at Home; Divorce Case Dismissals Soar Here Since September 11," *Houston Chronicle*, 25 September 2001, A1.

LASTING RELATIONSHIPS ARE BUILT ON SELFLESSNESS

spectacle, the flowers, the music, the attention-grabbing minutiae that can make such a happy event ridiculously stressful—and focusing more on the union itself.[3] For a few weeks, at least, we got our priorities straight.

Has it lasted? Are we still as focused on community and giving than we are on ourselves? Not really. But a number of images from the tragedy are forever imprinted in our minds. We'll always remember the planes and the fire and the smoke and the devastation and the images of fear. But I'm also choosing to remember the small silver linings that glimmered briefly through the dust, the instant and impulsive acts of community. Firefighters embracing. Volunteers lining up to search for victims. Neighborhoods gathering to cheer rescue workers. Churches scheduling interfaith prayer meetings on the fly. For a few weeks, New York City—the last place on earth we'd have expected—became a model of sacrifice, and our nation followed its lead.

Moral of the story: It can be done. Our natural tilt toward self-centeredness can, at times, tip the other way.

And if it can occur on a national level, how difficult can it be to lean that direction within our most important relationships? Not as hard as you'd think. It's as simple as learning to dance.

Have you ever seen a couple that really knows how to dance? The ones who have all the steps memorized and move in flawless parallel to each other? I'm talking about real dancing. Not booty-shaking or the eighth-grade hands-on-his-shoulders mutual sway, but the kind with traditional choreography and parallel movement, like the waltz, the tango, even the jitterbug. Couples who can dance together rule the parquet floor and are a joy to watch, even when they're dodging numbskulls like me whose dance steps consist of a modified Electric Slide step-shuffle coupled with a leftover routine or two from *Breakin'*.[4]

---

[3] Katharine Q. Sellye, "Tragedy Shifts Focus of Weddings," *New York Times*, October 14, 2001, national edition, A21.

[4] *Breakin'*: the quintessential film of the burgeoning 1984 hip-hop/dance scene, in which a struggling jazz dancer teams up with breakdancers Turbo and Ozone to win a competition against their nemesis, Electro Rock. *Breakin'* was the *8 Mile* of 1984. I loved it, but being eleven years old at the time, I was easily impressed. You should see it, though, if only for the climactic break-off, which was emceed by a then-unknown Ice-T.

Why are we so entranced by good dancers? Because during the dance, two individuals move fluidly as one. Building on a foundation of music and rhythm and coordination, they merge into a seamless, confident two-person partnership. There's little room for improvised rump-waggling or any degree of one-upmanship. Dancing is inherently selfless, as both dancers must work together to achieve a thing of beauty. One leads and the other is willing to be led, but each one surrenders—literally—to the arms of another.

With that image in mind, let's consider marriage. Like polished dancers, a relationship characterized by self-sacrifice can be a thing of beauty: a husband giving his wife a foot rub following a long day at the office without even being asked. A wife allowing her husband time to relax on Saturday before mentioning the garbage and the leaky faucet and the overgrown lawn. Planning a vacation just for him or a bed-and-breakfast weekend for her. Assuming a chore that usually belongs to your spouse. Taking care of the kids for an entire evening.

What about dating relationships? Sometimes selflessness is best displayed through the simple choreography of kindness and courtesy. Opening the car or restaurant door for your date—whether male or female. Choosing his favorite place to eat. Taking her to a movie you'll undoubtedly hate, but she's bound to love. Watching *Monday Night Football* with him. Watching *Trading Spaces* with her. Making eye contact. Offering nonsexual affection. Asking questions of your companion instead of talking about yourself. Listening.

Selflessness is an increasingly rare dance step, but when done right, there's nothing more inspiring.

There's just one caveat: The commitment to selflessness within a relationship must be mutual. Otherwise, you've got one butt-ugly dance. Fred Astaire was known for his remarkable grace, but if Ginger Rogers kept insisting on scrapping their routines to do the Cabbage Patch, the result would have been bizarre, if not downright hideous. Freddie, despite his polished elegance, would have looked bad due to proximity alone. It takes two to tango.

So there you have it—mystery dumplings, September 11, and

Ginger Rogers busting out like an extra in a Kid 'n' Play video—all employed to enforce a single point: Relationships fail when any two individuals refuse to consider the needs of the other. Relationships succeed when the pendulum swings the other way, when thoughts of one's own rewards are set aside for the benefit of someone else. When we offer to pay for a single dumpling. When we express our gratitude instead of scarfing down the free stuff. When me is replaced with us.

Here's one more thing you should know by now: Selflessness is reciprocal. Put someone else's needs ahead of your own, and they're likely to return the favor. A selfless attitude is as blissfully contagious as a yawn. Everyone wins, and no one has to choke down mud dumplings. It's good for me, it's good for you, it's good for BigHead Wang.

THE VALUE OF STORIES

5

When I was a kid, I thought I knew my grandfather. Paw-Paw had a broad nose and a neck crisscrossed with wrinkles. He smelled like a combination of the minty Copenhagen he dipped and the dry sawdust of his workshop. He built stuff, and he had all kinds of tools, and he had dentures, too. We would laugh and laugh when he took his teeth out. He watched the Today show during breakfast and listened to Paul Harvey at lunch. He sang a barrel-deep bass.

I thought I knew Paw-Paw, until around the age of twelve when I attended an air show with him. One of the aircraft on display was an old, World War II-era B-17 Bomber, the legendary "flying fortress." Paw-Paw took me aboard. As we climbed inside, he began to tell me about the plane: where the bombs were stored and how they were released, where the guns were stationed and the size of the bullets, what kinds of missions the planes flew and in what theaters.

"How do you know so much about this airplane?" I asked from the back of the fuselage.

"Because I was sitting right about where you are when we got shot down." I'm sure my eyes grew as wide as Paw-Paw's nose, but he kept talking.

"The wings caught fire, and the heat was about to weld the door shut. I couldn't see anything because of the smoke. So I backed up right there"—he pointed to the fuselage wall opposite the hatch through which we'd just entered— "and I jumped at the door with

both feet. Went right through and started falling until I remembered to open my parachute." He looked away, toward the front of
the plane, his voice dropping an octave. "Most of my buddies
died."

Based in Italy, my grandfather was on one of his last bombing
runs as a twenty-one-year-old side-gunner and flight engineer
when his plane encountered enemy fire over Austria. After reluc-
tantly bailing from his post—and his plane—he parachuted directly
into Nazi territory, where he was accosted by an elderly farmer
with a trembling rifle. Paw-Paw ended up in a succession of
German prisoner-of-war camps. He spent more than a year in cap-
tivity, subsisting on watery "stew" and thinking he'd never see his
family again. He held on mentally by reading and rereading a
bundle of letters from his bride, Mary Ellen, whom he'd left
behind in Hollis, Oklahoma.

His escape came as suddenly as his capture. Paw-Paw and a number of other prisoners were eventually herded out of the camp
and forced into a cross-country trek during the tail-end of winter,
in temperatures so cold he had to set fire to his precious letters to
keep his fingers from freezing. "I reckon it was intended to be our
death march," he said. After two weeks of retreating from Allied
forces, staggering across the countryside, the captors and prisoners eventually neared the Germany-Poland border. Without warning, a Jeep crested the hill ahead of them, driven by a British
colonel who'd become lost and accidentally veered into enemy
territory. Paw-Paw's German guards assumed it was the lead vehicle in an Allied onslaught, and they fled. The prisoners stood
there stunned, alone and shivering. Fear had stumbled into freedom. They'd been liberated by a Brit's bad navigation.

I thought I knew Paw-Paw until I heard him tell this story inside
the hollow shell of a vintage airplane. His version is usually punc-
tuated with much greater detail than above, buttressed by his
unique self-deprecating humor and colored, occasionally, with
pathos. Still, he tells it rarely. It's a powerful story, but a difficult
one—he didn't speak of those events at all until many years after
the war. I realize now there is much I don't know about my
grandfather. The man I do know was made during those months
as a POW, during that march, upon that liberation. To know Paw-
Paw is to know his story.

Ever since the earliest tribes first squatted around a fire, stories have been our connection to one another. They are the lifeblood of our culture. They help us understand one another. They illustrate who we are. They shape who we will become.

Next time you're at an office party or backyard barbecue, look around. Who has an audience? Who commands the group's attention? Here's a hint: It's not the guy near the grill trying to impress with collections of facts. Nor is it the one pushing a political agenda. Nope. It's the storyteller, the one who reveals himself, his history, his experiences to the group by way of adventure. He entertains us, and we feel most comfortable in his presence—because in knowing part of his story, we feel we know a part of him.

Good employees, good friends, good leaders—all have learned to appreciate one another's stories. Here's what they know:

Stories help us relate.

A 1998 article in *The New York Times* detailed the results of an Internet study by Carnegie-Mellon University. The researchers hooked up 169 individuals in Pittsburgh with free computers and Internet service beginning in 1995. The participants answered a series of questions at the start of the study, then again a couple of years later. The questions measured social contacts, depression, stress, and loneliness. You can see the punch line coming from a mile away: In this, the first real study of the social and psychological effects of home Internet usage, the researchers found that people who spend even a handful of hours online have higher levels of loneliness than those who use the computer less frequently. According to the article, the research raised "troubling questions about the nature of virtual communication and the disembodied relationships found in cyberspace."[1]

Via the Internet, those study participants undoubtedly came into contact with more people than they had previously—that's one of

---

[1] Amy Harmon, "Sad, Lonely World Discovered in Cyberspace," *New York Times* (August 30, 1998) A3. Though the results of this study are telling, the research itself may be flawed. A sample of 169 is hardly broad enough to merit the melodramatic title given it by the newspaper. And no indication is made as to whether the participants were already depressed and lonely to begin with. After all, Pittsburgh *can* be dreary.

the benefits of online communities. But what was the depth of that contact? Was it limited to trite message board chatter? Hastily scrawled e-mails? Vitriolic screeds? Useless variations on "Hi. How R U?"

It's a matter of quality over quantity. What's the social element missing from online activity? It's the power of stories to build and sustain relationships. The problem in today's society is that we've conceded the reins of storytelling over to the media. The plush cineplex and the ever-widening television screen have replaced the dinner table (the campfire of the fifties and sixties) as the primary forum for stories. That's fine on one hand; some are better storytellers than others, and their voices should be heard. What's not so good is that the human element is missing. You can't interact with a movie (unless it's *The Rocky Horror Picture Show*, but that's another, um, story).

It's not insignificant that one of history's greatest teachers and builders of relationships, Jesus, understood the value of shared experiences. In proclaiming His good news, He could have electrified His audience with impassioned preaching and theology. He could have pounded them with Scripture and lists of rules. Instead, He talked of the common things people could relate to, the images they understood from daily life: wheat and wine, yeast and dough, Samaritans and sons, pearls and swine. Jesus captured His audience with story. In turn, His story captured the world.

STORIES HELP US RESPECT.

One of my regular accounts at work is a local retirement community, for which I've written and designed a number of marketing materials. Many of these have been editorial profiles of that community's active residents and volunteers, men and women whose past experiences never cease to surprise me. There's nothing more fun than the transformation of a demure grandmother into a storytelling force when asked about her childhood. Any boundaries of time are demolished when photo albums are produced or heirlooms inquired about. I've met frail widows who flew for the Civilian Air Force. I've spoken with stooped men who have shaken the hands of presidents. I've profiled inventors, business pioneers, and authors, including one eighty-year-old woman who wrote dozens of pulp westerns during the sixties and seventies under a masculine pseudonym. When I first met these individuals, they were little more than names, room numbers, nursing home residents, or retirees. When the interviews were over, they had become inspirations.

It's easy to feel uncomfortable around people who are different from you—the elderly, the sick, the foreign. At the same time, that discomfort is largely based on the unfamiliar. Whether we admit it or not, we shy away from the unknown. We see a face, a skin tone, a collection of wrinkles, and we construct a one-dimensional character sketch of a person—bitter, dangerous, senile—to inject information into the void.

But if we stop there, we're guilty of prejudice. We must continue. When we ask questions and listen to the answers, that discomfort begins to decrease, and the unknown becomes known. Stories humanize us; they help us relate. They break through our caricatures and snap judgments. Guarantee: You'd find it much harder to ignore the old lady in the wheelchair at the nursing home if you knew she'd been the oldest sister of seven boys, a high school speech teacher, a former homecoming queen and the first female deacon at a Baptist church. With that knowledge of her story, you've encountered what's real, and discarded the flimsy structure your imagination built. That's respect.

STORIES HELP US REMEMBER.

It is said that each generation shares at least one common story— one that, in some way or another, serves to define and unite that generation. For our grandparents, that story is the attack on Pearl Harbor and the war years that followed. For our parents, it was the Kennedy assassination. For us, of course, our common story was written on the eleventh day of September in 2001. Standing at work that morning—1,500 miles away, on the skyscraper-free High Plains of Texas—my co-workers and I stared at the one television set in our building, shocked and unsteady, unsafe, uncertain. As the magnitude of the disaster began to materialize, I had the strangest thought: "Remember this. This is where you were when it happened." I looked around, recorded the faces in the room with me, the slant of sunlight through the windows, the dust on the TV screen.

Why? Because I knew it would be a chapter in my story, and an important one. Most of what I now know about my grandfather wasn't revealed to me that day at the air show, but a few years later on a Saturday afternoon. It was during my junior year of high school, and I was finishing an assignment for my U.S. History class. The assignment: Ask someone where they were and how they felt upon hearing that Pearl Harbor had been bombed, and record their answer. I asked Paw-Paw. His answer: "I was in Hollis, on the farm. I was angry. I enlisted the next morning." That statement was followed by two hours of story—and revelation. I met Paw-Paw that afternoon.

I'm hoping that one day, in the future, my three-year-old daughter will ask me where I was, and what I was doing, and how I felt on September 11, 2001. Because I know what I will tell her. I remember even the tiniest, non-essential details of that day. We all do, because that story belongs to our generation. Though painful, that wound is part of who we are, and someday, we'll need to let the next generation touch the scars.

Prolific author and activist Elie Wiesel, a Jewish survivor of the Nazi death camps, has spent his life telling the excruciating story of his people. In the prologue to his Holocaust novel, *The Gates of the Forest*, Wiesel relates the following traditional tale. It's a good closing thought:

> When the founder of Hasidic Judaism, the great Rabbi Israel Shem Tov, saw misfortune threatening the Jews, it was his custom to go into a certain part of the forest to meditate. There he would light a fire, say a special prayer, and the miracle would be accomplished and the misfortune averted.
>
> Later, when his disciple, the celebrated Maggid of Mezritch, had occasion, for the same reason, to intercede with heaven, he would go to the same place in the forest and say: "Master of the Universe, listen! I do not know how to light the fire, but I am still able to say the prayer," and again the miracle would be accomplished.
>
> Still later, Rabbi Moshe-leib of Sasov, in order to save his people once more, would go into the forest and say, "I do not know how to light the fire. I

do not know the prayer, but I know the place, and this must be suffcient." It was sufficient, and the miracle was accomplished.

Then it fell to Rabbi Israel of Rizhin to overcome misfortune. Sitting in his armchair, his head in his hands, he spoke to God: "I am unable to light the fire, and I do not know the prayer, and I cannot even find the place in the forest. All I can do is to tell the story, and this must be sufficient."

And it was sufficient.

For God made man because He loves stories.[2]

---

[2] Elie Wiesel, *The Gates of the Forest*, translated by Frances Frenaye (New York: Holt, Rinehart and Winston, 1966), prologue.

6

BEWARE THE URBAN LEGEND

So ... I had a bad day once.

I was driving at night on a business trip to Las Vegas. From some distance, a car was approaching. I was lucky to have seen it in the first place, because the vehicle didn't have its headlights on. Thoughtful driver that I am, I gave it the quick, "Hey, genius, turn your lights on," headlight flash as the car passed by. No sooner had I done that, the darkened vehicle executed a sudden U-turn and latched on to my tail like sweat on Springsteen. Perhaps they wanted to thank me for my good deed, but I have a feeling they intended to kill me as some sort of gang initiation.

Just my luck.

As the villains approached me from behind, attempting to pass, they suddenly switched on their brights and jerked back behind me, swerving wildly. I gulped, white-knuckling the steering wheel. Then they did it again: Lights. Tailgating. Honking. Beginning to suspect some sort of danger, I checked the rearview mirror and caught the glint of a butcher knife behind my head. Yikes! There was a deranged killer rising up from my backseat to stab me! Those thoughtful tailgating gangbangers and their high beams had been keeping me safe.

I stopped at a deserted gas station to let the killer out, and the rest of the drive passed without incident. I soon made it to my destination and proceeded to check into the hotel. I lugged my bag into the elevator, but was a little unnerved to see a well-dressed black man and his menacing entourage step in after me. "Hit the floor," he said to me. Fearing robbery or worse, I obeyed, dropping face-down upon the lushly carpeted elevator floor. The men started laughing, and I was helped to my feet. "What I meant to say was, 'Please press the button for the next floor,'" he said. "By the way, silly, my name's Eddie Murphy. Can I get you some flowers?"

Well, I felt sheepish, so I headed for the hotel's bar to take the edge off. As luck would have it, I encountered a shapely young blonde sitting alone. Asking if I could join her, we struck up a conversation and immediately hit it off. Over the next couple of hours, we shared several drinks together. I must have blacked out at some point, because suddenly I awoke in the bathtub of my hotel room, naked and surrounded by ice. So naturally I checked my e-mail. "Don't move," an urgent message read. "Call 911 immediately. P.S.—We've got your kidneys. Bill Gates has promised us one thousand dollars for each one we deliver to him, plus a trip to Disney World. Forward this to everyone you know. This is not a hoax."

Blasted organ harvesters.

You know all the stirring thoughts in the last chapter about the value of Stories with a capital S? Meet its dysfunctional cousin, the urban legend. If life is a party, then Story is its debonair host. But Urban Legend? He's the gangly, Ritalin®-deprived, bouncing-off-the-wall drunk, the guy with the spiked hair and sloppy drink—or vice versa. He's entertaining, he gives us all a good laugh, he's good for a water cooler recap the next day, but take him seriously? Um, no.

In our generation, during which IM has replaced the teenage slumber party and e-mail the campfire, urban legends have become the stitches of our social fabric. They show up everywhere, from movies and television shows to our Outlook® inboxes. When told correctly, with supplemental flair and dramatic pause, they can—best-case scenario—win you a captive audience. More likely, they can catapult you straight to dorkhood with the forward of a chain e-mail. "This may be too good to be true," you write ahead of a description of Bill Gates' charitable e-mail tracking request, "but what if it's not?!?!?"

The answer, of course, is this: If it seems to good to be true, then you should have recognized it prior to outing yourself as a gullible cornball. So, my fellow folklorists, here's something you should know by now: how to recognize the urban legend. Subtitle: How Not to Be An Inbox-Clogging Goof.

WHAT IT IS

You know what it is, but you may not realize it. An urban legend is simply a fictional story passed from one person to another and told as if true (i.e., this really happened—a friend of a friend swears on it!). The federal tax on e-mail? Urban legend. Kurt Vonnegut's graduation speech about sunscreen? Urban legend. The Neiman Marcus cookie recipe, HIV-infected needles in pay phones, the anti-religious misdeeds of Madalyn Murray O'Hair? Urban legends all.[1]

While a legend itself may be grounded in truth, it's either too good or too horrible or too funny to be real. For instance, the embarrassing elevator encounter with an African-American celebrity (who, depending on the era, has been identified as Reggie Jackson, Eddie Murphy, Michael Jordan, or even the ever-intimidating Michael Jackson) might have once been based on an actual occurrence of racial misunderstanding, but has long since passed into the realm of apocrypha. Others are just plain false to begin with—the headlight-induced gang initiation has no basis in reality, except for a copycat incident a few years ago back in Kansas. Same goes for the e-mail tracking programs promising trips to Disney World, clothing from the Gap or gift certificates for Outback Steakhouse. To be honest, whether it's true or not doesn't really matter as far as urban legend classification is concerned. What matters is that a story is alleged to be true without any real evidence. And the "this really happened to a friend" disclaimer? Sorry. Doesn't count.[2]

Urban legends fall into the category of *folklore*, defined as the traditional beliefs, superstitions and tales of the common people, disseminated through oral or written communication (as opposed

---

[1] Some purists require an urban legend to be an actual story with a cast or characters and a recognizable plot, and therefore consider e-mail virus hoaxes and odd facts or beliefs to be categorized as contemporary lore—but not actual urban legends. For our purposes, though, I'm inaccurately referring to all contemporary folktales as urban legends. It's simpler that way. So there.

[2] An interesting sidebar to the Eddie Murphy/elevator scenario: In 1996, Murphy recounted the story to *Parade* magazine, explaining that it never happened. According to the interview, the responses to his denial always amazed him: "But it *is* true," the doubters would contend. "My cousin was there." Considering all the cousins and friends and relatives alleged to have been present at the time, that was one humongous elevator.

to mass media). These legends tend to evolve into different animals during the telling; as a story is passed from one individual to another, each storyteller may add or drop certain aspects as needed. Therefore, the details change, the locations change, even the characters may change. That's how the organ harvesters were able to move so quickly from their New Orleans operation (sorry, pun intended) to Las Vegas in the well-known tale.

WHAT IT LOOKS LIKE

As mentioned in the previous chapter, the stories we tell are like societal glue. They supply common ground, helping us to stay connected despite differences in age, background, and worldview. Urban legends fill a particular niche by adhering to a handful of implied thematic elements—horror, humor, warning, embarrassment, and sympathy, to name a few—that reflect our shared concerns or confirm our pre-existing beliefs.

The best urban legends contain more than one of these elements. Consider the classic "Surprise Party" story. I heard this one during my freshman year of college; the storyteller was a student at Southwestern Baptist Theological Seminary. According to her, this happened to an engaged couple one of her friends supposedly knew:

> Two seminary students met and fell in love during their first year at SWBTS and had recently become engaged. They went out to dinner a few weeks after the engagement to celebrate her birthday. After dessert, they decided to stop by her parents' house for a sweater. No one was there, and—despite their chosen career paths—one premarital thing led to another. Long story short, they ended up naked and fooling around upstairs. Pretty soon the phone rang; it was the girl's mother. Mom wanted her to go downstairs and set the VCR for her favorite show. Still feeling playful (and still quite unclothed) the guy suggested a piggyback ride for his naked fiancé. She hopped onto his shoulders, he started down the stairs, and as the two of them reached the bottom the lights clicked

on. A host of people yelled, "Surprise!" The two
naughty seminarians were surrounded by their
best friends, fellow church members, and the girl's
parents. Uh-oh. The engagement was eventually
called off, and neither finished their education.

Upon first hearing this one, I believed it—what a great story! Then
I heard it again the next summer, from a different source. In that
retelling, the protagonists weren't from the seminary, but were a
recently married pastor and his wife. Coincidence? I began to have
my doubts. Then I heard it again a couple of years ago, and this
version starred a naked boyfriend and girlfriend who were sent
into the basement to turn off the clothes dryer, where they were
surprised by a party. At this point, I knew I'd been had by a quintessential urban legend, one with all the standard elements.

Primarily, "The Surprise Party" is a cautionary tale, one that uses
its lurid details to teach us a moral lesson: that premarital hanky-
panky has negative consequences. See what happens when you
(ahem) count the chickens before they hatch? But wait, there's
more! We've got humor: What's funnier than a naked piggyback
into a room full of your closest friends? We've got embarrassment:
What's worse than a naked piggyback smack into the up-close-
and-personal scrutiny of your future in-laws? And some versions
of the story even include horror. In the final account I heard—the
one with the boyfriend/girlfriend and the clothes dryer—the
female ended up having a nervous breakdown.

Most urban legends contain one or more of these thematic touch-
stones. The best ones contain them all, tying everything together
at the end with a you-won't-believe-it twist.

WHERE IT COMES FROM

An urban legend, very simply, comes from someone you know.
While the story itself might be outlandish, the teller usually isn't.
It's someone you trust, and she swears up and down that this
really happened to her friend's uncle or to the receptionist at her
dad's office or to somebody her neighbor knows. What reason do
you have to doubt? Answer: plenty.

Regardless of his or her storytelling prowess, no one wants to begin a good story with, "So I heard this from my friend Sean who heard it from his dentist who swears this happened to the friend of a cousin of an old Army buddy of his." That's way too bulky. Instead we streamline the intro—"This happened to a guy Sean knows"—giving the impression that we're only a step or two away from the event itself, when actually we're hundreds or even thousands of people removed. The surprise party story that supposedly happened to someone my friend knew? Turns out it's been making the rounds since the 1920s.[3]

Just as the teller plays a large role in the believability of the urban legend, so does the story itself. The really juicy legends are chock-full of detail—this didn't just happen to somebody somewhere, but to engaged students at Southwestern. The would-be rapists knocking women unconscious with sniffs from perfume bottles were last noted at the mall right down the street. The story in your inbox about a nine-year-old girl who's "been missing for two weeks" provides the girl's name, her mother's name, their hometown and even a contact e-mail. It's hard to imagine it being completely fabricated, right?

For this reason, some urban legends even make their way into newspapers and TV newscasts. Long-time radio personality Paul Harvey has been a consistent vendor of exaggerated stories, but who would dare to distrust the voice of a generation? We can hardly get through life harboring blanket distrust of the media and our friends, so our natural tendency is to believe what we're told.

Our own psyches are also culprits in our gullibility. Why do horror stories and cautionary sex tales show up so often in urban legends? Because those are the kinds of things we think about. We fear disease, sexual deviance, and public embarrassment. We worry about kidnappings, gang violence, and contaminated food. We distrust the government and large corporations. We're afraid of—evidently—kidney thieves. In previous centuries, people were terrified of the deep, dark woods (home to dangerous creatures), and this apprehension found its way into their folktales. Consider *Little Red Riding Hood*, *Snow White*, *Hansel and Gretel*.

---

[3] This according to urban legend experts David and Barbara Mikkelson, who operate the highly informative Urban Legend Reference Pages at *www.snopes.com*. For more on the "Surprise Party" story, see *www.snopes.com/sex/caught/surpart1.htm*.

You undoubtedly noticed the proliferation of e-mail hoaxes and legends following the September 11 terrorist attacks. The "stay out of the malls on Halloween" warnings, the faked "unlucky tourist" photo, the one about the guy who survived by surfing the rubble as the towers fell, the false Nostradamus prophecies—all of these rose from the dust of lower Manhattan as we attempted to cope with real-life horror. We were looking to find comfort, to place blame, to assign meaning, and the urban legends that resulted—however harmful or disrespectful or just plain stupid they were—helped us in some way to muddle through.

WHERE IT'S GOING

Unlike history, which involves accurate research and written communication, the urban legend falls in the category of oral tradition, the transfer of stories via word of mouth. From the Iliad and Odyssey to the Bible and the Talmud, oral tradition has been vital to human interaction for thousands of years. Folklore and fairy tales are prime examples.

Urban legends are the folklore of today. But instead of telling each other stories over the campfire or dinner table, as we once did, we now find ourselves spreading them via the click of the mouse. Contemporary folklore can now reach thousands of "listeners" in a matter of seconds, simply by forwarding e-mail. It requires no effort or judgment on our part, nor does it require even the basic ability to communicate. Regardless, folklore has flourished in the last ten years like no other time in the history of the world. So does this lead to a boom in creativity? A utopia of cultural understanding? A swarm of excellent storytellers? Um ... no. Instead it leads to a hard drive stuffed full of virus hoaxes, faked photos, computer scams, and useless petitions—crap we're far too willing to pass on with a quick click, just in case it's true.

It's usually not. Seriously—it's not true, particularly when the e-mail begins "This is not a hoax" (which is like prefacing a boast with "I don't mean to brag" or gossip with "Not to talk bad about people, but ...").[4] On one hand, our technology has made us all a lot more informed about our world. On the other hand, it's turned

---

[4] Or, since we're on the subject, a professional athlete who insists, "It's not about the money."

us into a bunch of easily fleeced forwarders of computer virus warnings.

So what's the answer? Do we dismiss every cautionary e-mail as a hoax? Well, not exactly. Some are legitimate warnings describing such digital scourges as the mass-mailing "Bugbear" worm or the Gibe virus that cleverly disguised itself as a Microsoft security update e-mail. But most of the other frantic alarms are deliberately false. You've no doubt heard their names: A (Virtual) Card for You, WTC Survivor, It Takes Guts to Say Jesus.

Here's the problem, though: Deciding to ignore every virus warning that comes across your desktop could be harmful. And knee-jerk forwarding of every panicky virus warning can be annoying. So what do you do? It's simple: Do your homework. Go to school by checking out the "Computers" section of the valuable Urban Legends Reference Pages at Snopes.com, which regularly posts updates—along with "real vs. hoax" ratings—of the e-mails currently making the rounds. Another excellent resource is the Urban Legends and Folklore site at About.com. These sites can generally tell you whether a warning is real within a click or two. So next time you have the urge to mass-forward, take a deep breath, steady your itchy trigger finger and play it smart. You do not have to mindlessly obey the "Pass this along to EVERYONE you know" line. Pass it along to the trash instead. Web users the world over will thank you. So will everyone you know.

But if you encounter a too-good-to-be-true story? A tale of kidney-gutting horror or hook-handed killers or bodies under the bed? By all means, enjoy it. Embellish. Have fun. Make it your own. Say it really happened—*no, seriously, really!*—to your sister's tattooist or your mom's parole officer. Spin a clever yarn. Remember, by passing along an honest-to-goodness urban legend, you're contributing to a greater good. You're preserving our culture through oral tradition. Because if each of us fails to do our part, the generations to follow will grow up having never heard about Richard Gere and the gerbil.

And that, friends, would be truly shameful.

7

OPTIMISM IS BETTER THAN PESSIMISM

There once was a set of identical twins named Pete and Perry. Despite appearances to the contrary, the boys were complete opposites, particularly in terms of their emotional outlook. Pete was a full-fledged optimist, always looking on the bright side. He awoke each morning fully expecting to see the sunshine, ace all his tests, and, while he was at it, win the lottery. He didn't seem to notice failures and went through life chipper as a bluebird. The other kids found him annoying.

Perry, a card-carrying pessimist, was as fun as a bowl of oatmeal. Regardless of the situation, Perry could be expected to assume the gloomiest view possible. He went through life calculating his chances of, for instance, being flattened by a bus or contracting a deadly virus. That kind of thing happened in movies, and Perry figured it was just a matter of time before it happened to him, too. As you might expect, the other kids didn't like *him* much either.

The boys' parents worried about them and their lack of meaningful friendships, which they were certain could be traced to the twins' unbalanced emotional states. And, for that matter, they were tired of Pete's chirpy "good mornings" at 6 A.M. and the way Perry always said "this might be goodbye forever" when they dropped him off at school. So they took the boys to a psychiatrist.

He suggested a unique plan to balance the boys' personalities and outlined a crafty strategy for the parents to follow. "On the twins' next birthday, put them in separate rooms to open their gifts," he told Mom and Dad. "Give the pessimist the best toys you can afford, and give the optimist a really big box of manure."

"Manure?" they asked.

The psychiatrist nodded his head thoughtfully.

Mom and Dad followed his advice, and when Pete and Perry's birthday arrived, put the plan in motion. They listened as Perry started opening his first present. "A computer," he said, less than thrilled. "This'll be out-of-date the minute I turn it on. It's probably loaded with viruses already." He continued to the other gifts, sighing as he unwrapped each one: "A PlayStation is nice, but I'll never be any good at these games. I might as well not even hook it up. A new baseball glove? How long until I miss the ball and it hits me in the eye? I'll probably end up blind and brain-damaged."

The parents then tiptoed across the hallway to check on Pete and his nicely wrapped box of dung. The smell hit them as they cracked the door, and they were shocked at what they saw: Pete was covered in the manure, digging feverishly through the box and slinging crap across the room. "You can't fool me!" he said, laughing amid the filth. "Where there's this much poop, there's gotta be a pony!"[1]

The M. Night Shyamalan thriller, *Signs*, showed us that there are two kinds of people in the world: Those who view the events of life as signs and miracles and those who believe in luck and coincidence. That kind of oversimplified dichotomy may be fairly plausible—it certainly worked within the context of Shyamalan's screenplay—but I think there's probably a more accurate way to divide the world in two: optimists and pessimists.

Each of us has a natural tendency to view the events of our lives through a certain lens. It's the traditional glass-is-half-full or half-empty philosophy—we either nod our heads along with Pete or identify with Perry. The twins' dung scenario is a little exaggerated, perhaps, so let's examine a more true-to-life situation.

Let's pretend you're a good, hard-working employee, and upon arriving at work on Monday you happen to pass by your boss in the hallway. "Good morning," Mr. Bossman says. "I need to talk to

---

[1] Brian Cavanaugh, "The Optimist," *Condensed Chicken Soup for the Soul*, Jack Canfield and Mark Victor Hansen, Eds. (New York: Health Communications, 1996), 118-119. Cavanaugh's story, originally published in *More Sower's Seeds: Second Planting* (Mahwah, NJ: Paulist Press, 1992), has been adapted and greatly expanded for our purposes here.

you about something. Come by my office after you get settled in."

Now—what's your first thought? If you're a pessimist, you'll automatically turn apprehensive, back-scanning the last few days in order to figure out what you might have done wrong. *Is my boss going to fire me? Did I screw up the last project? Is this because of all the personal e-mails? Do they know about the stickie-notes I took home?* To the pessimist, everything is his fault; everything is cause for worry. When something bad occurs—even something ambiguously bad, like a vague statement from a supervisor—he assumes the worst. He broods. His energy decreases. His health suffers, and he may eventually become clinically depressed.

The optimist's thought process following the Bossman encounter swings the other way: *He wants to tell me how good a job I did on the Daniels account,* our optimist may think. *He's going to promote me. Maybe I'm getting a raise. Maybe I'm getting a bigger office.* For one thing, the optimist doesn't automatically consider the worst-case scenario, but rather, assumes a more positive outcome. When actual obstacles do arise, they're rarely a big deal. Such challenges are simply extra hurdles in the race. The optimist may be surprised by the hurdle and stumble a little, but she picks herself up and starts running again.

The line between optimism and pessimism is not hard and fast. Few of us are entirely one or the other; there are hardly any true Pollyannas in the world, just as there are few who can out-Ebenezer Scrooge. Most of us fall somewhere in between the fictional Pete and Perry, and our response to a difficult situation can fluctuate from one side to the other depending on the week, the season of the year, the way we feel physically, and even how we started our day. You knew this was coming, but here's something you should know by now: Optimism is better than pessimism.

"Thank you," you're saying with mock astonishment and oozing sarcasm. "That's quite the newsflash, Geraldo. You're forgetting that you can't just suddenly make yourself into an optimist. Some people are wired to think negatively from the beginning, right?"

Right. Some people do have naturally optimistic or pessimistic tendencies, though most of us are more inclined to the latter than the former. In fact, we might as well consider low-frequency thoughts of pessimism to be normal. But, just because we're knee-deep in negativity doesn't mean we can't escape it. Pessimism doesn't have to be permanent: You can get rid of it piece-by-piece, like stripping bark from a tree. It's a slow process, but it's necessary for a well-lived life.

In *Learned Optimism*, a 1991 bestseller, the well-regarded psychologist and clinician Martin E.P. Seligman details the roles optimism and pessimism play in regards to quality of life, having studied both viewpoints for decades. It is his belief that who we are—and what we become—are deeply related to how we explain life's stumbling blocks to ourselves. He writes: "The defining characteristic of pessimists is that they tend to believe bad events will last a long time, will undermine everything they do, and are their own fault. The optimists, who are confronted with the same hard knocks of this world, think about misfortune in the opposite way. They tend to believe defeat is just a temporary setback ... Confronted by a bad situation, they perceive it as a challenge and try harder."[2]

The most efficient way to move from pessimism to optimism is through what Dr. Seligman calls "explanatory style"—protecting yourself against failure or crisis by interpreting it in the most positive light. In the workplace example above, the comment by the boss elicited different explanations in the pessimist and optimist—both of whom, we're assuming, are valued employees. The pessimist begins allowing one unpleasant scenario after another—being fired, failing at a project, even being caught at marginally forbidden behavior—to career through his mind as an attempt to clarify the vague "meet my in my office" comment. His explanatory style is fueled by negative emotions like fear, failure, and guilt.

Meanwhile, the optimist is driving a different direction, one ruled by self-confidence and hopefulness. She expects the best, and doesn't allow herself to attach negative fallout to a neutral statement. If anything's out of the ordinary, she tells herself, it's the good kind of unordinary—and she fully expects to benefit from it.

Let's take another scenario: an unsuccessful date. As opposed to

---

[2] Martin E.P. Seligman, *Learned Optimism* (New York: Knopf, 1991), 4. I'm indebted to Seligman and his valuable insights for most of the good stuff in this chapter.

wild conjecture (anticipating a firing or promotion based upon a single comment), this situation has a known outcome—failure. You meet someone new and you go out, but for a variety of reasons, the two of you just don't connect. Both of you look great and perform admirably, but in the end, you both go home knowing it won't work out.

How you explain that failure to yourself says a lot about your personal outlook on life. The optimist will find positive reasons for the rejection. *He didn't seem comfortable with me,* she'll think. *He's not ready for a relationship right now. Or maybe he's more compatible with a different personality type.* She could even take it a step further: *Perhaps I intimidated him. I was simply too smart, too charming. He's just too stupid to know how great I am. Anyway, we didn't click, but that's because of him, not me.*

The pessimist, however, internalizes the rejection. *She didn't seem comfortable with me,* he'll think. Then he mentally dropkicks himself, blaming her discomfort on something he did wrong. Maybe he had bad breath. He must have been a dull conversationalist. His appearance was below average and, well, maybe just he chose the wrong activity, or the wrong clothing, or the wrong companion. Whatever the reason, it was his fault.

In explaining the unsuccessful date to herself, the optimist refused to accept a negative rationale. When one came up mentally, she argued against it. Not so the pessimist. He failed to dispute his internal dialogue, allowed a downbeat analysis of the date to run its course, and ended up attributing the bad experience entirely to his own shortcomings. After the date was over, each of them ran into a wall—*he/she didn't seem comfortable with me*—but approached it differently. The pessimist saw the wall, recognized it (he's been here before) and just stopped. He turned around and went home, failing to continue the race. The optimist got to the wall, stopped momentarily, then began to climb. Thinking of constructive reasons why the date didn't go well, she eventually reached the top, dropped to the other side, and started moving again. She'll run a good race. The pessimist never gets past that wall of failure because he always accepts the first natural explanation—"maybe something's wrong with me"—and never argues it away.

When confronted with a failure or difficulty, the optimist explains it in three ways, according to Seligman.

1) She depersonalizes it. The failed date is about his issues or circumstances, but has little to do with her.

2) She judges it as temporary. While that specific date may have gone poorly, that doesn't mean every date will be bad.

3) She identifies it as specific. This guy, for some reason, didn't match up properly with me. But it won't be true of all guys everywhere.

The pessimist does the opposite; his explanatory style is self-defeating. He personalizes it ("It's my fault"). He thinks it's a permanent problem ("All of my dates end up this way"). And he thinks the problem is pervasive ("There must be something wrong with me"). With this kind of outlook, every failure can be a devastating blow to his self-esteem.[3]

The solution is to learn to anticipate the negative explanations of defeat and turn from them when they inevitably arrive—for pessimists, these thoughts can be automatic and show up so quickly they aren't challenged. But if you know they're on the way following a failure, you can prepare to combat them. How? Gather evidence against your self-defeating thoughts. When "it's my fault" starts to emerge after the date, shut it out by remembering the people who do like you, who find you interesting, who enjoy being around you. Then, like the optimist in the dating example above, come up with different explanations for the failure (i.e. "He's not ready for a relationship right now") and use it as a basis for arguing with the bad thoughts. Finally, says Seligman, try to distract yourself from the pessimistic thoughts. Some people keep regurgitating the negative explanations like an anti-mantra—*something's wrong with me, something's wrong with me*—and before long, they believe it. When those thoughts arrive, set them aside. Take that thought captive and lock it away somewhere. Find something else to occupy your mind.

---

[3] These are explained in full by Seligman, 76-77, and throughout *Learned Optimism*.

The goal is not only to take charge of what you think, but also to control when you think it.[4]

The reasons to live as an optimist are many. For one thing, you're more fun to be around—we'd all rather hang out with Tigger than Eeyore. Secondly, evidence suggests you'll live longer. A recent study by the Mayo Clinic found that people with a negative outlook on life have shorter life spans than those with positive attitudes. In fact, people who scored high on optimism in a specially-designed personality test were discovered to have a 50 percent lower risk of premature death than those with a more pessimistic score. Researchers also discovered a number of other health benefits related to optimism, such as fewer work- or activity-disrupting physical or emotional problems; higher pain tolerance; increased energy; and natural feelings of peace, calm, and contentment.[5]

So, nutshell chapter synopsis: Optimism is good, but negative thoughts sometimes come naturally. With some practice, though, you can argue those negative thoughts away, and learn to look at the bright side. As a result, you'll live longer and feel better than all the downbeat party poopers out there. And speaking of poop, never never never give your kid a box of excrement for his birthday. Because he just might mistake it for a pony, and teasing a child like that is cruel.

---

[4] Seligman, 89-90.

[5] "What's Your Outlook? The Benefits of Positive Thinking," *Mayo Clinic: Healthy Living Center: Healthy Aging Center* (Posted September 18, 2002, at *www.mayoclinic.com/findinformation/ healthylivingcenter/index.cfm*).

THE FINANCIAL

FINANCIAL PROCRASTINATION WILL EAT YOU FOR LUNCH 8

"My friend Winnie is a procrastinator. He didn't get his birthmark until he was eight years old."—Stephen Wright

In 1984, a woman in St. Louis observed a handful of bees buzzing around the attic vent on her two-story home. It was just a few—nothing to worry about—so she shrugged off the problem. Over the summer, she occasionally noticed a few more bees flying in and out of the attic, and kept telling herself she ought to have it looked at. Still, she remained unconcerned. Then one day, toward the end of the season, everything fell apart. Literally. After months of gradual bee proliferation, the whole attic had become an enormous hive; the ceiling of her second-floor bedroom caved in under the weight of hundreds of pounds of honey and an army of angry bees. She narrowly escaped injury. Her home wasn't so lucky.

So let that be a lesson to you—too much honey can be dangerous. So can procrastination.

Almost all of us have had to deal with some form of procrastination over the years. Waiting until the last minute to begin term papers. Starting to write that book report (or even read the book) at a quarter-to-midnight the day before it's due. Building up fines because we can't seem to find the time to return *Goonies* to Blockbuster. Getting the car inspected in May when the sticker expired in February. Filing our taxes.

Oooooh—taxes. Let's stop right there.

For most of us, long-delayed school assignments are in the past. An overdue inspection sticker, while technically against the law, is only a big deal if you get pulled over. And who doesn't have time to watch another round of *Goonies*? (Put your hands down.) That kind of procrastinating—while not exactly responsible—is relatively harmless. Live and learn, right?

But the *financial* kind of procrastination? That's something entirely different. It's the cranberry juice stain on your carpet that won't go away. You can cover it up for a while with an area rug or creatively reposition your couch, but the stain's not gonna disappear on its own. It'll be there forever, at least until you replace the carpet.

And as long as we're talkin' metaphor, let's say the cranberry stain keeps getting worse. It doesn't just set; it spreads. Before long it creeps beyond the edge of the couch. Then it oozes onto your couch, jumps across the coffee table to the wall, and drips down your high-definition wall-mount plasma TV. Soon, your stuff is irrelevant. All you know is the stain.

That's why financial procrastination is a big deal—a big, fat, expensive deal—because you can be a victim of its effects over a long period of time. Why? Because Granddad was right: time = money. And waiting too long to make good financial choices can screw you over for years to come. The longer you put it off, the bigger the hive.

So here's something you should know: When it comes to finances, do not postpone the big decisions just because you're still young and carefree. You're likely to end up old and poor. Following are some things to consider before the honey starts leaking into the light fixtures.

DEVELOPING A BUDGET

First of all, let's not use the word "budget." It's loaded with negative baggage—from governmental pork to the overbearing husband who gives his wife an envelope full of twenties each month and says, "This is what you get. Don't ask for more." Smart financially, dumb relationally. I side with financial speaker and author Deborah Knuckey, who prefers the phrase "spending plan."[1]

---

[1] Knuckey is the author of *The MsSpent Money Guide: Get More of What You Want with What You Earn* (Hoboken, NJ: John Wiley & Sons, 2001).

Without any kind of spending plan, people end up buying stuff and paying bills willy-nilly. The money goes to whatever they want ("It was on sale! It would be sinful not to buy it!"), with the leftovers applied toward paying the bills. That's pretty fun at first: no stress, lots of stuff. Who wouldn't benefit from an extra ski jacket, anyway? Unfortunately, this "system" can bottom-out quickly, when you reach the point where there's no money left to pay the bills (fortunately for you, you'll have all those ski jackets to wear after the gas company turns off your heat). By then, of course, it's too late. You resort to credit cards, fall prey to the minimum monthly payments, wince as the interest kicks in, and suddenly the wide road toward debt stretches before you like I-40 through western New Mexico. Barren. Forbidding. Desolate.

And that's before you hit the desert.

Learning to live on a budget—oops, sorry, a *spending plan*—is something many people discover a bounced check too late. It requires discipline and planning. It means giving up the impulse-buy high that consumers thrive on. But if money is consistently tight and bill payments are consistently late, there's no more important step to take financially. Make a plan while you're young, stick to it religiously, and life will be easier.

Start by listing all your expenses during an average month. This includes basic needs (rent, food, car, insurance, utilities, etc.) as well as unexpected or irregular expenditures like visits to the dentist or household repairs. I'd also include retirement savings in this category. If you want, you can even figure in an amount for frivolous stuff like shoe sales at the mall, movies, extra cheese on your burritos—whatever squeezes your toothpaste. Add those up, then compare them with your monthly cash flow. Take into account every penny you'll make from stable sources of income, including salary, part-time wages, interest from savings account, cash from Grandma (you leech), and anything else you can depend on month-to-month. Don't consider irregular sources of income such as bonuses, overtime pay or birthday gifts. Then compare your two lists: net expenditures vs. net income.

Let's say your net expenditures for each month are $2,500. Your monthly take-home income is three thousand dollars. For the budget-conscious, that means all but five hundred dollars each month is designated toward something specific. The rest is "free" spending money. So does that mean you can go and blow it on Ding-Dongs and YooHoo? Not necessarily. I'd suggest saving as much of it as you can—everyone should have some emergency money stashed away in an easily accessed savings account, just in case. That way, you're never floored by the unexpected, like a car wreck, a hard drive failure, or even a layoff.

Finally, once you've set your budget, stick to it. Get it through your brain that when an amount of money is designated toward a regular expenditure, it's gone. The cash may still be in your checking account, but you can't touch it. That's the one rule to making and keeping a budget: Don't flex when it comes to concrete items. It may be okay to draw from your entertainment or clothing budget to cover an unforeseen expense, but you cannot steal from the money set aside for rent just because FunJet is offering a special to Vegas.

So start planning your spending now. Make it routine. It may be a little painful at first, but like any habit, you'll get to where you don't even notice it. Without a budget, you spend too much, buy stuff you don't need, and put yourself at risk. With a budget, you get your bills paid on time, you grow your savings, and you even have something left over at the end of the month—something besides a pile of past-due bills.

PLANNING FOR RETIREMENT

For most of us, retirement is at least forty years away. That's a spouse, a house, two kids, tuition, and maybe a few grandchildren down the road. Way too far into the future to even consider, right? Why sock away a hundred dollars a month when those dollars could be spent on, say, the new digital two-way microbrowser/meat thermometer that everyone at work is packing? Or why save something you won't use for decades when you're not even sure you can make rent next week?

We can always come up with reasons not to do something. Lack of time. Lack of ability. Lack of understanding. But in the case of retirement planning, every month you procrastinate costs you big time. That hundred dollars you can't afford to save this month? Forty years from now, that's five thousand dollars. Big difference.

This is explained in greater detail in the 401(k) chapter, but you need to understand—today, while you're young—the value of compounded interest and how it works in saving for retirement. Let's say you sell your collection of Boba Fett paraphernalia on eBay and net $10,000 from it (nice collection, dork). You decide to forgo the new gadgets and invest the money instead. Very smart. If you invest that ten grand at the age of thirty-five and average 10 percent interest, you'll see that sum grow to $175,000 by the time you're sixty-five. (Of course, in this economy, 10 percent interest is a pipe dream, but indulge me here—it's a good round number.) At any rate, that's decent money.

But what if you made that investment ten years earlier? Take the same amount—ten thousand dollars—and invest it at twenty-five years old instead of thirty-five. Multiply it by the same interest, only this time it grows ten extra years. By the time you're sixty-five, you'll have over $450,000 in the bank. That's nearly three hundred grand extra, just for starting earlier.

If time = money, then procrastination = lots less money.

Don't put off saving for retirement any longer. If your company offers a 401(k), contribute as much as you can, particularly if your employer also offers a match. If not, set up a regular or Roth IRA and start saving. Every little bit counts. Regardless of the monthly contribution or even the interest rate, you'll do tons better by starting now than if you wait a few more years or even months. Put time on your side. Bite into the juicy fruits of compounded interest.

PAYING OFF DEBT

It happens to everybody. Sometimes credit cards and uncontrolled spending are the culprits. Maybe it's car trouble or a medical emergency. In many cases, it's school loans. Everyone carries a little bit of debt. Most financial experts even recommend it (as a mortgage) when it comes to home ownership. But for some people, debt can get out of hand. A couple of missed Visa payments. A home improvement loan, a trip to Europe, a blown transmission. And before you know it, a few hundred dollars of debt have ballooned into a few thousand. Not good.

The easiest way to fall into debt is to live above your means via the improper use of credit cards. The temptation is powerful: Buy what you want, whip out the Platinum, and make the minimum payment until you can find the funds to cover it. No harm, no foul—until you consider that, after subtracting your minimum payment, the balance of your credit card account is subjected to exorbitant interest in the realm of 18, 19, even 20 percent and above. Here's the really scary part. Throw a few hundred bucks on the card, start making minimum payments, and you'll never—never—pay the card off. Give it a few years of unhindered growth, and it'll reach hive-like proportions. When it falls through the floor, it'll bring your credit history down with it. And a bad credit history can hang around a long, long time.

So if you've amassed any debt at all, most experts will tell you paying down that debt (unless it's a home mortgage) should be your primary goal. Procrastinators often procrastinate because a task or project seems too overwhelming to even think about tackling. Imagine David feeling that way about Goliath.

Instead, focus on the details. Take a few small steps. David gathered five smooth stones from a nearby river. You can select your smallest debt (maybe a gas card account) and get it paid off first. When that's done, move on to the next one. Save money. Sell stuff you don't need. Compare prices. Anything extra you have each month goes to debt payment.

Soon, your small steps will have slammed your debt between the eyes, and not a moment too soon.

Procrastination is a guaranteed way to lose money, whether it's the retirement savings you missed out on or the debt you let yourself slip into. It's tempting to pass off these worries as irrelevant to someone at your stage of life—retirement is for old people, budgeting is for accountants and dads—but don't give in. Start now, and save yourself the trouble. Financial freedom starts with discipline, but it ends with peace. And long, restful nights. And light-blue belted jumpsuits, but maybe that's just my granddad.

IT PAYS TO LIVE BENEATH YOUR MEANS

9

In 1992, former Canadian advertising executive Kalle Lasn began a brave attack on a powerful enemy: North American consumerism. The founder of *Adbusters magazine*, Lasn was fed up with the culture of overconsumption in which he found himself. So, naturally, he did what most of us would do. He created a holiday.

And it wasn't just any holiday. Lasn brainstormed, implemented and began promoting an event called "International Buy Nothing Day." He staged it on the biggest shopping day of the year, the Friday after Thanksgiving. He asked his supporters and fellow celebrants to participate with him by, in fact, not participating—to literally buy nothing for twenty-four hours. He gave them simple instructions: Stay home. Buy nothing at all. Don't go shopping. Take your lunch to work instead of buying it. Take a thermos instead of buying coffee or tea. Walk to work instead of buying gas. Find a way to do without for just twenty-four hours.

Since then, Lasn and friends have celebrated and campaigned for Buy Nothing Day on an annual basis, even going so far as to attempt to place what they call an "uncommercial"—one asking its viewers not to buy products—on network television. Every year, the anti-ad is rejected by ABC, NBC, and CBS. Only CNN Headline News, to this point, has allowed it on the air. (Remarkably, Lasn's group doesn't intend the ad to be a public service announcement—they're trying to *purchase* airtime. The networks keep turning down a paying customer because they aren't comfortable with the message.)

Lasn has found a way to make a lot of people uncomfortable; that's what happens when your ideas hit below the belt.[1] He has a

---

[1] For more on Lasn and his culture-jamming guerilla tactics, read "Kalle Lasn Is Mad As Heck and Isn't Going to Take It Anymore," written by the late Donella Meadows at *The Global Citizen* (*iisd1.iisd.ca/pcdf/meadows/KalleLasn.html*).

problem with our nation's consumer culture, with our compulsive need to shop, with our tendency to purchase things we don't need to make ourselves feel good, to impress each other. Behind him is this statistic, adhering to the ever-reliable 80/20 rule: The developed and wealthy Western nations, which comprise 20 percent of the world's population, consume more than 80 percent of its natural resources.[2]

Buy Nothing Day has turned into an interesting social phenomenon, as environmental extremists lock arms with evangelistic Christians, Mennonites with media watchdogs, all to make a cultural statement: "Enough is enough."

I'm here to proudly tell you that I have participated with them every year since this "holiday from spending" began. Are my hackles raised by American overspending? Yes, of course. Well, maybe a little. Actually, I just don't like crowds, don't like the mall, and don't like shopping. So you won't catch me near any combination of those on the day after Thanksgiving, mind-blowing sales or not. I'll have nothing of it.

But Lasn and the Adbusters team do have a very valid point: We buy too much stuff. Not because we need it. Sometimes, not because we even want it. We buy because we can. It's an extraordinarily stupid mindset.

Let's consider the people closest to you—your friends, your fellow employees, your family. What forms the foundation for those relationships? What's the joint that keeps them together? No one I know would seriously chalk the connection up to material things: "I'm friends with Jessica because she has a cool car." Or "I like to spend time with my parents on account of their fantastic antique furniture."

Possessions don't matter nearly as much as we think they do, and that's why I think Buy Nothing Day is a great idea—if only to

[2] The so-called "80/20 principle" has long been described by economists and behavioral researchers. It theorizes that, in any situation, approximately 80 percent of the work will be done by 20 percent of the participants. For example, in most societies, 20 percent of criminals commit 80 percent of the crimes. See Richard Koch, *The 80/20 Principle: The Art of Achieving More with Less* (New York: Bantam, 1998).

remind us of that simple truth for twenty-four hours. Inherent in that idea is a financial virtue too many of our generation have failed to adopt: the art of living beneath your means. The importance of doing so is something you should know by now.

It's estimated that 80 percent of America's self-made millionaires—by which we mean those who have pulled themselves up by their bootstraps, rather than being born into money or having it given to them because they can throw a ninety-seven-mile-an-hour fastball left-handed—have achieved economic independence by being frugal. They're rich because they don't spend much money. They buy only what they need, and then, only what they can afford.

I can't tell you how many people I know who do the opposite, living above their means. Here's how it happens: Joe graduates from college, finds a nice job with a company looking for energetic young talent, and begins earning a decent salary. So Joe, who's earning more now than he ever has in his life, does the obvious—he goes out and buys himself a brand-new car. He didn't exactly need one, as his 1993 Civic got him to and from work just fine, and with good fuel economy. No, Joe made the purchase simply because he suddenly had the money for it. Because a hotshot young businessman really shouldn't be driving around in an old Honda, should he?

So is Joe wrong? Not necessarily. Is what he did morally repugnant? To some, maybe, but not to me. Is it smart? Well, no. Generally speaking, it's not smart.

Why? Because most people like Joe don't stop with just the car. Soon they fall in love with someone else their age, someone with an equally nice job and nice car. The two of them pool their money, grin at how much they're both raking in, and began to live the DINK lifestyle—Double-Income, No Kids. They buy the biggest and newest house they can afford. They outfit it just like page thirty-two of the Pottery Barn catalog. They get used to eating out and start paying too much for entertainment.

Then they decide to have kids, and when Junior finally arrives, they're in a bind.

More and more young mothers these days are opting to become

full-time, stay-at-home moms. Many of these want to—really, really want to—but can't, because they're living above their double-income means. For these young families, cutting back to one income is absolutely impossible without a drastic lifestyle change. So they shell out thousands a year to put the kid in daycare, because they can't afford to do anything else.

When a lifestyle of consumerism starts impacting your family, that's a pretty good signal that things need to change. It's hard, because our spending habits are a part of us—they began to develop as soon as we received and cashed our first paycheck. Many of us have been on the road to financial trouble for a long time, but there's no need to keep driving when we know the destination won't be any fun. It's time to consider getting off at the next exit, and the best strategy for this is to adopt a frame of mind that's not always popular in today's culture—insistence on spending less than you make. Here's how you do it:

1) Budget your spending. Decide what kind of standard of living you want to adopt and figure out how much money it will take to do so. Make sure that amount is less than what you earn. Stick to it, and save or invest whatever remains. If you bring home $3,000 a month, budget for $2,500. The rest goes in the bank.

2) Think before spending. Consider your future before making a big financial decision, particularly when buying cars or houses. A thirty-year mortgage is a looooong time. You may be able to afford it now on a dual income, but do you always want to be dependent on that income? If you're married and planning to have kids, this is extremely important to consider.

3) Cut expenses. Do you really need two soft drinks everyday? That tall cup of mocha? Another pair of Skechers? You'd be amazed how little we can live on comfortably. You don't have to be a monk, but you don't have to live like royalty either. Find a few areas—the non-necessities like entertainment, dining out, or name-brand clothing—where you can cut back. Then do it.

4) Hide the gravy. This is a game my little sister used
    to play at the dinner table, but it has financial appli-
    cations as well. Say you're making thirty thousand
    dollars a year and living comfortably on that. Then
    you get a five thousand dollar raise. Do you go out
    immediately and lease a bigger apartment? Do you
    buy a new car? Do you blow it on a vacation? No.
    Instead, "hide" the money. Set up an automatic
    withdrawal with your bank, then direct deposit the
    extra into a retirement plan or mutual fund. You
    haven't needed it thus far, so why blow it just
    because it's there? It's gravy. Bring home as much
    bacon as you can and put it in the freezer for later
    use. Do this for a few years, and you'll be in better
    financial shape than you could have ever imagined.

The secret to living beneath our means is to question everything
we spend money on, from discretionary stuff like gym memberships to the basics like food and shelter. Ask yourself: Do I really
need this, or do I just want it? Question frequently and answer
honestly, and you're on your way to capping consumerism.

There's nothing wrong, of course, with making money. It's a
necessity, so go ahead—set whatever financial goals you want to,
then work hard to get there. Earn as much as you can, but remember: If you're accustomed to spending more than you make, then
it doesn't matter what numbers are on your paycheck—you'll
always fall a little short of your goals.

Then, every year as you're trying to button your turkey-challenged
pants the day after Thanksgiving, pause to consider what day it is:
International Buy Nothing Day. Relax. Stay at home, and feel good
about yourself. Not just because you're refusing to participate in
unthinking consumerism for a day, but because you've made it a
lifestyle.

If that's the case, you're different from most of us. Be proud.

10

YOUR 401(K) SHOULD BE AGGRESSIVE BUT DIVERSIFIED

"Everybody needs money! That's why they call it money!" —Danny
DeVito (Mickey Bergman) in *Heist*

No, I'm not entirely sure what the above quote means either, but
it comes from David Mamet's labyrinthine double-cross caper,
Heist, starring DeVito and Gene Hackman. In it, Hackman's character, a soon-to-retire thief, complains to DeVito's discount crime
boss that he doesn't want to do one last job because he,
Hackman, doesn't need any more money. DeVito's response—
"Everyone needs money! That's why they call it money!"—has
inspired nearly as much conjecture, praise, and deconstruction
among film critics as Rosebud in *Citizen Kane*.

To some, it's the funniest line ever written, rat-a-tat perfection. To
others, it's gibberish, the same old Mametian tough-guy dialogue
that sounds clever without saying anything. To most, it's just a
throwaway line about money. But try using it next time you get
into a financial discussion. Enjoy the looks on your friends' faces
as they attempt to understand what you just said. They won't.
That's why they call it money.

The same kind of faux intelligence, confusion, and suspicion
exists these days when the pundits—in this case, financial, rather
than cultural—start talking about a no less controversial category
of money: 401(k) plans. As of this writing, the stock market is still
down and the consensus is still out. Will the Dow pick back up?
Will it dip deeper into recession? Stabilize within the year? Enter
into a slow but steady growth period? No one knows.

Advice for investors is as varied as the stock ticker. No one dis-
putes that investing, as a general practice, is the only way to keep
pace with inflation and build a decent amount of money over

time. But no one seems to agree where to invest. Do enough research and you can find any number of theories. Buy stocks while they're low. Stick to bonds because they're safer. Focus on index funds. International funds. Technology funds. Buy and hold. Sell and bolt.

What everyone does know, in this war-worried, post-Enron, scandal-of-the-month economy, is that, while 401(k) plans need some serious debugging, they are still the best choice for the young investor. That's you, dear reader, so listen up.

First off, I don't want to assume that everyone is up-to-date on the theoretical virtues of the 401(k). If you know how it works, skip the next few paragraphs. If you're more of an investment virgin, read on.

At your request, the company you work for can set aside a portion of your paycheck (this is called an "elective contribution") into a separate fund to help you save for retirement. Many employers will match part of your elective contribution up to a certain amount (for instance, a common corporate match is 50 percent of your contribution up to 6 percent of your salary). You pay no federal income tax on any contributions to your 401(k) or any income earned by those contributions (which is, by all accounts, an excellent benefit) until you collect on the plan, which you aren't allowed to do until you're at least fifty-nine and a half years old. You'll find this is pretty much the only time in life when your half-birthday means anything.

The money you set aside is combined with your company's match and used to purchase a variety of stocks, bonds, and money market investments. You'll usually have a bunch of options, each varying according to risk level and growth potential. You choose an investment approach, elect a certain amount to be taken from your paycheck, and watch your nest egg grow.

It's that easy, especially if you start while you're young. Consider this example. Bob graduates from college, knocks around between Prague and the Kho Sahn Road for a couple of years, then comes back to the States at twenty-four. He then gets a good post-graduation job paying more than thirty thousand dollars a year. Because he's single and has few financial responsibilities, he decides to put back a lot into his 401(k). Combining his monthly contributions with his employer match, Bob ends up investing a total of $250 a month into his retirement plan. That's three thousand dollars a year. Good job, Bob!

If Bob continues this trend for forty years, until the age of sixty-five, guess how much money he'll have? Assuming such variables as regular monthly contributions, no withdrawals or loans, 8 percent interest compounded monthly (which, even in the economy of the last year, is still a pretty reasonable long-term figure), and tax-deferred earnings, Bob can plan on an account balance of nearly nine hundred thousand dollars. Total amount invested? One hundred and twenty thousand dollars, part of which came from his employer.

Behold the power of compounded interest. See? Your twelfth-grade economics teacher was right.[1]

That's why, even in a volatile market, 401(k) plans are a good idea for the young investor. But since most plans give you different options for distributing your money, the hard part is knowing what kind of strategy to pursue. So here's something you should know by now: Experts almost always advise young investors to be both aggressive and diversified in building their retirement portfolios. What does that mean? Read on.

BE AGGRESSIVE

You're young. College is over, a new career is beckoning, and you're bringing in a steady paycheck. Retirement is as distant as Johnny Knoxville from normal. Why get caught up thinking about life at sixty-five if you don't even know what you're doing next Saturday? Right?

Wrong. Now is the perfect time to plan for the future. Doesn't mean you need to start test-driving Winnebagos or eating at Golden Corral, but you do need to come up with a retirement

---

[1] For those of you who slept through twelfth-grade economics, compounded interest refers to the process of gaining interest on interest. In other words, the interest you earn on your investments is re-invested, which then allows you to earn interest on interest. Thus, your investment keeps building and building upon itself, and before you know it, you've got a potload of money.

strategy and stick to it. Don't wait. The sooner you start, the more time your money has to grow.

One way to be aggressive is to enroll for your 401(k) as soon as you're qualified (many companies require employees to work a certain number of months before eligibility kicks in). Using Bob's example above, the difference between starting at age twenty-five and starting at age thirty is just fifteen thousand dollars in total investments, but three hundred thousand dollars in accumulated interest. Those last five years of compounding are big. Shaquille O'Neal big. Lace up your investing shoes and get in the game as quickly as you can.

The second step in aggressive investing is to contribute each month until you bleed. Maximize your plan—defer as much to your 401(k) as your employer will match. A common mistake employees make is failing to take advantage of their company match, not realizing that, in effect, the bigwigs are pretty much shoving free money into your account. We've already stated that some employers match 50 percent of contributions up to 6 percent of your salary. If that's the case, don't just set aside a paltry 2 or 3 percent. Scratch as much out of your employer as you can. Fork over 6 percent to get the full match. Then, just because your employer stops there doesn't mean you have to—you can give more, up to 15 percent of your income or twelve thousand dollars.[2] The extra money each year won't be matched, but it does add up—a little bit year-to-year, a truckload decade-to-decade. Just ask Bob.

Step three in being aggressive involves your investment choices. Most 401(k) plans let you decide where to invest your money. You'll have several options. An easy way to evaluate investment options is by a simple risk/reward ratio. Aggressive, high-risk investments give you the opportunity for higher potential reward. Conservative, low-risk investments have less potential for growth, but let you sleep better at night.

---

[2] This is the cap for 2003, an amount set by the IRS and adjusted annually to reflect cost-of-living increases. It's currently set to increase by one thousand dollars every year until 2006. Your employer should keep you informed each time the amount changes. If they don't, let me know. I'll see what I can do.

Microsoft Chairman Bill Gates, who has a few dollars to his name, once said he only looks at the price of Microsoft stock once a month—his focus is on the end game, not what's immediately in front of him. Same goes for investors in their twenties and early thirties. At this stage, your 401(k) is still in development mode; you're trying to build it up. For that reason, you should be willing to accept greater risk in exchange for a higher growth potential, because you won't be needing the money for at least thirty years. So even if a certain stock or fund tanks for a year, you're still okay. Chances are very likely things will even out over the long haul.[3]

The rule for investors under forty is to be brave. Invest aggressively. This kind of strategy involves what is usually called a "growth portfolio." Such a plan is diversified among different types of stocks (which tend to fluctuate), with very few, if any, investments in more stable bonds and cash instruments. Growth funds maximize your investment over the long-term, but can sometimes look ugly in the short-term—especially during a struggling economy. But history shows that, over the decades, the stock market will rise slowly but surely, despite the inevitable hiccups. Here's a tip: Put your money in, check it a month at a time rather than daily, and make sure you're nicely diversified. Which brings us, in a dazzling segue, to the next point ...

DIVERSIFY

Roger Boyce, an Enron employee living in Minneapolis, believed in the energy giant so much he put all of his 401(k) contributions into Enron stock. He got bonuses of Enron stock. His company match came in the form of stock. He lived and breathed and sweated Enron stock. And for several years, this living and breathing and sweating made him rich. He retired a millionaire. Then, when Enron collapsed, his $2 million portfolio dropped like an egg to a tile floor. The result was messy. Within days, it was worth

---

[3] Or, you could work at Enron, or Lucent, or WorldCom, or Tyco, or some other high-tech bust—and lose it all. Some companies offer a variety of funds to choose from, and make their company match in straight-up cash. Unfortunately, others match with company stock, often refusing to let employees sell until they reach a certain age (such as fifty-five). That's no worry when the stock is doubling or tripling in value, but it's a big problem when the stock falls to pieces and your nest egg gets scrambled.

less than ten thousand dollars.[4] The Enron lesson: Eggs are fragile, and sometimes they break. Don't keep them all in one basket.

The weird thing is, few working Americans seem to have learned much from Enron and horror stories like Boyce's. According to the Employee Benefit Research Institute in Washington, D.C., employees at publicly held firms that offer company stock as a retirement option still have at least 30 percent of their money invested there. Early in 2002, there was some huffing and puffing in Congress to pass laws to regulate this in some way. Enron workers were paraded around telling their riches-to-rags stories, but then the television cameras disappeared and very little resulted. Governmental regulation isn't out of the picture, but experts say not to expect much.

The cure for the problem is up to you—you must diversify your portfolio. Please note: Diversification does not mean investing in a cluster of different instruments (a few bucks in stocks, a few in bonds, a few in mutual funds). Rather, diversification means to invest across and between different sectors of the marketplace. Choose a variety of stocks instead of one single stock. Don't over invest in a certain class of mutual fund (small caps, for instance) or fund sector (technology, energy). Spread your investments out—make sure they represent a cross-section of options.

A good way to diversify is to include among your investments an index fund and an international growth fund. An index fund tries to match the return of a specified market index, usually the S&P500. Over the last few years, index funds have regularly outperformed actively managed funds, which try to beat the market, but don't always succeed (often charging higher fees in the process). An international fund manages a diversified portfolio of stock from companies located outside the U.S. (thereby ensuring at least part of your investment is not tied to the performance of the U.S. economy). I'd designate money toward one of each of the above if they're available, and then choose a couple more options, such as large-, mid-, or small-cap funds.

The goal is to broaden your investments. Diversify geography,

---

[4] Catherine Valenti, "Retirement at Risk? 401(k) Losses in Wake of Enron's Collapse Could Inspire Changes," ABCNews.com (posted December 4, 2001).

diversify industry sectors, diversify fund managers, diversify everything. Gather as many eggs as you can, but spread them over several baskets. That way, you'll survive major economic swings, industry downfalls, and bankrupt companies. Even if one basket drops, you've still got plenty to cook with. In closing, a brief list of things you need to know about your 401(k):

1) For young investors, there's no better way to plan for your retirement.

2) There's free money involved if your employer matches your contributions in some manner. Take advantage of it.

3) Start as early as possible. Extra years at the beginning equal extra years at the end, when, thanks to compounded interest, your money grows at a staggering rate.

4) Contribute as much as possible. More contributions mean a higher company match and a greater base for earning interest.

5) Invest smart. Be aggressive while you're young and go for the highest returns. But remember that higher returns come with higher risk, so you need to diversify. If your employer matches your contributions with company stock, then don't put any more of your money into that same stock. That's what happened with Enron. Don't let it happen again.

So there you go. Sign up for your 401(k) and start saving. Keep the above in mind, and you'll be ready to retire in only, um, forty years. Give or take. Woo hoo.

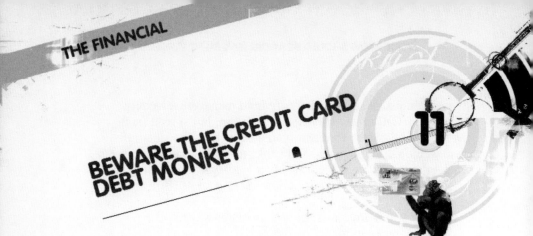

BEWARE THE CREDIT CARD DEBT MONKEY

11

Meet Tracy. Tracy is a college freshman. She's the middle child in a middle-class family from the suburbs of middle America. She did well in high school, graduated in the top 10 percent of her class, and got a couple of nice scholarships. Her grandparents are helping pay for some of her living expenses; the rest will be covered by student loans. Tracy, feeling grown-up and responsible, has promised to pay those loans back after graduation. She's a good girl, that Tracy.

The day she moved into her dorm—with Mom and Dad in tow—she ran into a gaggle of sensitive, scraggly-haired, ruggedly handsome upperclassmen handing out the first issues of the school newspaper. Tracy grabbed one, and a flyer tumbled out from the fold. "Free T-Shirts!" it said, just for signing up for a credit card! The shirts were lame, of course—who really wanted a bulky white tee with a bank logo on the front?—but it got Tracy's attention.

Boing: idea.

"Dad?" she said, playing the role of thoughtful college student with skillful aplomb. "I'm thinking about getting a credit card." Dad frowned, deep in thought, or possibly feeling indigestion from the egg and cheese biscuit he'd inhaled for breakfast.

Tracy didn't wait for an answer. "What if my car breaks down? What if granddad's check is late and I run out of cash? What if there's some kind of emergency?" She turned on the grown-up logic. "I don't want to always be calling you asking for money."

Dad sustained the frown, perhaps even deepening it. He sized up the fluorescent green flyer. An eternity passed. Fossils turned to oil. Carbon compressed into diamonds. Dick Clark discovered a gray hair. Finally, Dad's verdict: "Nope."

Tracy: "Seriously?"

"I'd rather you ask me for a couple bucks now," Dad explained, "than run the risk of you being thirty-thousand bucks in the hole in a few years. I've seen it happen. You're not ready for a credit card."

"I'm eighteen years old, Dad."

"I know people twice your age who can't handle a credit card. The answer is no. Not yet."

Tracy sulked, Dad popped a Maalox, and Mom wringed her hands. The rest of the day was awkward until they said their good-byes around 5 P.M. By 5:30, Tracy had completed the credit card application form and shoved it into a mailbox. After all, she was old enough to vote—surely she could handle a piece of plastic. She deserved more credit for that than Dad was willing to give. Besides, she told herself, it's just for emergencies.

Tracy's credit card and promotional T-shirt arrived the next Friday, just in time for the weekend. Her first emergency occurred less than twenty-four hours later. She and her two roommates were feeling homesick and, deciding to drown their sorrows in cheese, mushrooms, and black olives, stopped by the local pizza joint. After ordering, Tracy noticed—horror!—she'd left her checkbook in the dorm. Luckily she had her shiny new credit card. She decided to charge it and, feeling generous, picked up the entire tab. After all, that just meant a higher cash back bonus at the end of the year, right? "It's on me," Tracy said with a smile. Music swelled. The card gleamed in the neon light.

Four years later, Tracy's graduating with a 3.4 average, a degree in elementary education and a whopping eighteen-thousand-dollar credit debt spread over three different cards. She's also racked up nearly the same amount in student loans—loans, you'll recall, she promised to pay off. And the dorky T-shirt the credit card company sent her? She uses it to clean the bathroom.

Tracy's story is not unique. From 1999-2001, the average credit card debt among undergraduate students increased almost one thousand dollars. Nearly four out of every five students surveyed had at least one credit card to their name, and its average balance was more than $2,700.[1] That, my friends, is a whole lot of emergencies.

The fallout is that a lot of young people are leaving college and entering the workplace with a ferocious debt monkey clinging to their back, a financial burden that won't go away soon. The under-thirty-five set is the least likely to pay their bills in full each month. Combine that with an average student loan obligation of fifteen thousand dollars or so, and you've got an entire generation living on the financial edge for years to come.

It's not that we're financial idiots, or lazy mooches, or burdens to society—most twentysomethings are hard-working and focused on their careers. But saving for things like retirement or a future down payment on a home is hard enough as it is. And when debt is teetering over you like a cartoon anvil? *Imposible*, as my Spanish teacher used to say.

So here's something you should know by now: Credit cards can be dangerous. But you knew that already, right? If that's the case, then, we'll move on to something more appropriate: How to get out of debt.

THE CREDIT CARD CONUNDRUM

Credit card companies target college students for a simple reason. People are loyal to their first credit cards. Set the hook while they're in college, and you've got a cardholder for life. Unfortunately, the banks are pretty indiscriminate in who they go after. A Spring Break booth on the beach at Daytona isn't exactly targeting those with a certain income level or a good credit history. It's targeting anyone in a swimsuit.

The dilemma is that credit cards aren't inherently bad. When used properly, they can be a valuable financial tool. They're convenient for making big purchases or for shopping online. They're helpful

---

[1] Christine Dugas. "Debt Smothers Young Americans." *USA Today* February 11, 2001: 1-2A.

when renting a car or making a hotel reservation. And one of the best ways to establish a good credit history is by paying off a major credit card on time, every month.

But, as Jon Lovitz would say, *that's* the ticket: paying the entire balance month-by-month. That little "minimum payment" box is enticing, is it not? Book a cruise to the Yucatán, and all they want from you next month is ten dollars! You can enjoy it now and keep your wallet full until you have the cash to pay for it. It all sounds nice and wonderful, except for a little something called interest. You want numbers? Let's say your cruise costs one thousand dollars and your credit card interest rate is 18 percent (which is average). By making the minimum payments each month, it'll take you nineteen years to pay off the debt, by which time you'll have forked over nearly two thousand dollars *in interest alone* for a trip that cost half that to begin with. Gulp.

And if you miss a payment along the way? That stain will be on your credit report for years to come—something creditors, insurance companies, and even employers can peek at in order to determine your financial responsibility. The moral? A couple of bad credit card goof-ups can keep you from renting an apartment, buying a car, or getting a job.

You've heard it all before, of course. It's hardly news—and should be common sense—so I'll only say it once: If you're going to use a credit card, you need to use it wisely. Find one that gives you cash back bonuses or lets you collect airline mileage. Or at least find one that doesn't charge an annual fee.[2] Don't be late on payments. And if possible, only use it when you can cover the expense, when you can pay off your credit card bill in full at the end of each month. That's worth saying again: Pay off your credit card bill every month.

---

[2] Or, if you're already with a card that does charge a fee, take a stand. Customers who put a lot of purchases on their cards are held in high regard. The banks don't want to lose you. So call the customer service number and simply tell the operator you're not going to pay the annual fee. If they balk, tell them to cancel your account—you're gonna switch to a card without a fee (there are plenty of those out there, and they know it). Most of the time this'll get them nervous enough to waive your fee for the year. Seriously, this works. You'll probably have to do it on an annual basis, but why not? How many five-minute phone calls can net you fifty bucks?

HOW TO GET OUT OF DEBT

Of course, smart use of credit cards is often advice received too late. If you're already carrying a five thousand dollar balance, that's a secondary concern. The primary one? That 18 percent interest rate, compounded monthly. It's not going away by itself, so you'll have to take action. It's time to shake the debt monkey. Here's a few ways you can do it:

1) Suck it up and increase your payments. The minimum payment? That's what banks want you to pay—that prolongs their opportunity to charge you interest. The longer you take to pay off the balance, the more money they make. So start making payments now, as much as you can each month. Where's that money going to come from? Perhaps you need to look at your expenses—surely there's a luxury that can be curbed. From iced cappuccinos each morning to dinner out on the weekends, find something you can sacrifice to the gods of debt management (for tips, check out chapter nine on living beneath your means). Then take whatever money you save and apply it to your credit card balance. Dig deep, adjust your lifestyle and recognize the minimum payment for what it is: a legal way to put you in the hole.

2) Practice self-control. Don't put anything on your credit card that you're not going to pay off the next month. Otherwise, you're countering your own attempt at debt reduction. If you can't discipline yourself to do this religiously, then get out the scissors. Take a deep breath, then put the card out of its misery. Slice it up like a pizza. Cancel it, then resolve to pay cash for any purchases until you're out of debt. Otherwise, it's like complaining about your sunburn while lying naked on the beach. No one will feel sorry for you. But they will stare. After all, you're naked.

3) Beg. While you're working to pay down your debt, it wouldn't hurt to negotiate with your creditor for a

lower interest rate. Explain your situation to them, keeping in mind a couple of things creditors fear. Number one, they're afraid you might be tempted by another card company offering a lower rate (again, there are plenty of these out there), causing you to transfer your balance elsewhere and depriving them of all the juicy interest. Or number two, they're afraid you might declare bankruptcy as a last resort, leaving them open to a loss. As a result, many creditors will often go the extra mile in working with you. If they're sufficiently afraid you might bolt or bankrupt, you'll have plenty of leverage in asking for an easier repayment schedule or a lower interest rate. Give it a try—it doesn't hurt to ask. Sometimes it just depends on getting the right customer service operator on the right day.

By the way, if you're successful in lowering your interest rate, that doesn't mean you can lower your payments accordingly. Keep paying the same amount. That way, the money that used to go toward interest can now be applied to the principle—which makes the total debt load decrease faster.

4) Borrow. This is the tricky part, because it requires some serious thought and occasionally can introduce negative consequences. Still, paying off your debt with borrowed money is worth considering. Most of us have 401(k) plans, life insurance policies, or family and friends, each of which can be good sources for loans. I know what you're thinking: So, Mister Things-You-Should-Know-It-All, the best way to get out of debt is to get into more debt? The answer is a) Possibly, and b) I don't like your tone.

Here's the deal: Say you've got a five thousand dollar debt that's growing at an 18 percent interest rate. Very, very bad. Why not pay off the card by getting a loan at a lower interest rate? You'll still be in debt,

but the worst part—the interest—will be much less painful. A decent option is to borrow from your 401(k). Most plans will let you borrow a certain amount, at a rate a couple of points above prime—which, most of the time, is way cheaper than 18 percent.[3] Do your research, though, as some plans limit your borrowing abilities to important stuff like medical bills, education, or a first home—a couple years of willy-nilly college spending don't exactly fit the category.

An even better option is to borrow from friends or family, but to do it very cautiously. The really loving ones may give you an interest-free loan, but don't expect it—this is money that could be earning interest if they weren't such suckers for your woe-is-me story. Instead, tell them you'll pay a point or two over the prime interest rate, whatever it is at the time.[4] If you take this route, though, make things official. Sign a written agreement, establish a payback and interest schedule, then stick to it—disagreements over money can ruin friendships and tear apart families. Don't let this happen. Be kiss-their-feet grateful and remain utterly resolute in paying off the loan.

A FEW WORDS ABOUT DEBT CONSOLIDATION

If you've tried the above steps and are still struggling with debt, there's one more avenue you might consider. No, it's not bankruptcy. Bankruptcy is hardly worth it for someone in his or her

---

[3] Even better, the interest you pay on 401(k) loans eventually goes back into your own pocket—it goes into the borrowers account, not the lenders. *But* ... you'll have to repay this loan in five years or less, according to the rules. And should you switch jobs before paying it back, the loan must be repaid immediately or it will be considered a partial distribution of your funds. Since you're below fifty-nine and a half in age, that distribution will be taxed a 10 percent early withdrawal penalty. There can be major drawbacks to this strategy, so think about it first.

[4] The prime rate is the amount charged by banks to their customers with the best credit. The rate is almost always the same from bank to bank. For 2002, the rate held steady at 4.75 percent.

twenties. The stain on your credit history is too great and the need for it is too little, not to mention some of the ethical issues involved.[5]

A better option may be debt consolidation. Debt consolidators (also known as "credit counselors") are generally non-profit agencies that help you negotiate with creditors to get your debt in line.[6] They go over your expenses and help you decide what you can afford to pay each month—then they work with your creditors to merge unsecured debt (think credit cards or medical bills, but not mortgages or car loans) into a single payment. These non-profits can often negotiate lowered interest rates on your behalf, which allows you to pay more each month toward the principle.

Once the terms have been agreed upon, they'll help you set up a payment plan. You'll write just one check to them each month, and they'll disburse it to your creditors. And after you've set that up, the creditors are supposed to stop calling you.

It's actually a pretty good situation, but there's something you should be aware of: These non-profit companies actually work for the creditors. (Insert chilling organ music here). The debt problems in this country are so great and bankruptcy is so easy that many creditors are jittery about the losses they might realize when people default on their loans. So they make contributions to these non-profit credit counselors, which allows them a nice tax write-off. The two bedfellows then work together to keep your payments coming. It's a strange, near-incestuous relationship, but in many cases, everyone wins. You consolidate your debt and get lower interest rates, the nonprofit gets some nice contributions, and the creditor doesn't lose their shirt to another bankruptcy. The system breaks down in a few cases where the nonprofits start

---

[5] Young adults have fewer people dependent on their income. And unless they spend money like a lunatic, they've had less time to amass the monstrous bills that make bankruptcy a valid option. It's simple: for young people, bankruptcy should only be an option if debt is causing considerable mental distress—inability to sleep, severe depression, thoughts of suicide. In my opinion, bankruptcy for financial reasons is rarely justified for the young, unburdened consumer.

[6] But not all debt consolidation agencies are non-profits, and not all non-profits are there just to help. Non-profit status is just a way to organize a business. Some debt relief agencies aren't afraid to take advantage of your desperation by offering a quick fix. In short, they profit off your problems. Be cautious. Avoid agencies that require up-front fees or promote "payday" or title loans.

to make promises they can't keep, like repairing your credit history or wiping it completely clean. Um ... you can't do that, at least not legally. There are no do-overs in the land of credit history. The information on a credit report might as well be chiseled in stone, and the only way it can be altered is if you change your social security number—which, to put it bluntly, involves fraud. If a debt consolidator leads with this pitch, back away from the plate. You don't want these guys' help.

If everything's on the up-and-up, though, debt consolidation may be a viable option. Look into it, but be careful.

Credit cards are like dynamite. When used properly—in carefully controlled situations and for a specific purpose—they can be very helpful. When handled recklessly, though, that little piece of hologrammed plastic can be deadly. Because so many people have failed to recognize the danger of uncontrolled credit card use, credit debt has become a major problem in the U.S. Understanding how to use your credit card properly is one of the most important things you need to know.

And if you've already discovered that danger first hand and ended up burned, then getting out of debt is one of the most important things you need to do. It won't happen overnight. It requires tightening the belt and tailoring a budget (see page 53). It involves sacrifice and smart spending—whatever is necessary to help you make the biggest payments you can every month. It'll be a challenge, but you can do it. In fact, you *should* do it, and you should start now. The longer the debt monkey rides your back, the longer it takes to throw him off.

HOW TO CRAFT AN ATTENTION-GETTING RESUME

12

In the axiom-rich world of marketing, it's often said that a client is looking for one of two things—a solution to a problem or a good feeling. It's the kind of workplace cliché management gurus toss around like a superball, bouncing it off any and everything.

But they're right, of course. Good feelings and practical solutions are what we're all after. Doesn't matter if we're conscious of it or not—we almost always consider a form of these criteria during each decision-making process, whether we're evaluating a university professor or hiring a babysitter.

The same can be said for those employers who are wading through stacks of resumes in hopes of finding someone who can solve their problem (filling a vacant or new position) and give them a good feeling (filling a vacant or new position with an employee who will not steal Sharpies®).

So keep that in mind over the next few moments. Take a deep breath, strap on your safety harness and please keep your hands and feet inside the vehicle at all times—we're about to condense your entire life into a single letter-sized page (or maybe two, if you're lucky). It's called a resume, and how to effectively write and prepare one is something you should know by now.

WHAT IT IS

The French have given us a number of useful words and phrases that, over the years, have weaseled their way into the English language. The proper use of some of these borrowed words can make you sound intelligent: *bon vivant, nouveau riche, fait accompli.* Others trickle pleasantly off the tongue: *rendezvous,*

somersault, ricochet. But a handful of French words are absolutely no fun at all, adding neither class nor delight to a conversation. I'm thinking here of *tampon, nasal, dentist,* and of course, *résumé.*

The word "résumé" is a French term that means "to summarize." And that's literally what it is—a summary of who you are, a synopsis of why you should be hired. For the purposes of this discussion, though, I'd like to approach the resume from a different angle. Not as a summary or static list of achievements and experiences, but as an advertisement, a piece of salesmanship. It's a form of marketing. The subject? You.

WHAT IT NEEDS TO DO

Simply put, a resume needs to get attention—the good kind of attention—and hold it long enough for a prospective employer to pick up the phone and give you a call.

Here's how it works. Manager Jim is given a mandate from high up the corporate ladder. "Hire someone to fill the position, Jim," he is told by his boss. So Jim puts an ad in the paper, or posts a listing on a website: "Position available. Excellent blah, blah, blah. Looking for blah, blah, blah. Competitive blah. Send resumes to Jim."

So, four days later, Manager Jim finds himself peering over a stack of 243 resumes burning a hole in his coffee-stained desktop. The corporate suits are still pushing him to make a hire, so he's shuffling frantically through the pile. He's scanning, not reading anything in-depth. At most, he gives each resume about twenty seconds—ten seconds less than an average television ad—to make an impression.

Not all impressions are positive. For instance, Jim gets one resume that is typeset in a flowery, unreadable script. He squints at it for maybe three seconds before crumpling it up in frustration. Another grabs his attention because it's printed on fluorescent orange paper. The color makes him dizzy. "I'm not hiring circus clowns," he mutters, and refuses to read a word.

Then he gets to one that gives him pause, and this time it's in a good way. The page itself is clean and organized, but it does more than just inform him; it excites. It spurs him to action. He picks up the phone. He asks for an interview.

That's the purpose of a well-crafted resume: not to get you a job, but to secure an interview. It's your foot in the door. Problem is, there are usually lots of other people hoping to jam their Kenneth Coles through the same door at the same time. That's why you've got to do something to stand apart, to get noticed, to get invited in. You need a resume that will highlight your skills, sand over your splinters and boost you toward the job you've always wanted. Or at least the mailroom near the job you've always wanted. (After all, everyone has to start somewhere. Just ask Jim.)

Here are a few tips to help you get started:

EVEN THOUGH IT FEELS STUPID, WRITE AN OBJECTIVE

Start with your name and contact information (address, phone number, e-mail address). Center this part, put your name in all caps, and make it three or four type sizes larger than the body of the document.

After this comes the "objective" section of your resume—the short sentence that, for the most part, states "this is why I'm applying." It should be specifically targeted for the job for which you're applying. It needs to be quick and to-the-point: "A desktop operator position for a book publisher," or "An elementary-level teaching position for the Dallas Independent School District."

Some have argued that the objective is archaic and an unnecessary waste of space. I disagree.[1] This is the place to grab your reader by the nose from the start, by showing a) that you've researched the position or company and know what is being offered; and b) that you have a career direction and know precisely what you're looking for. In the example above, two-thirds of the

[1] The objective statement is worthwhile as long as it's specific to the job offered. Generalized, blanket statements like "A challenging position that will allow me to utilize my gifts and talents to contribute to the company while offering opportunities for growth and advancement" are worthless. The only purpose they serve is to indicate you didn't take the time to customize your resume, or that you have no idea what you want to do.

resumes Jim receives will be of the shotgun variety, from people who send a resume to every job listing they see. When Jim comes upon yours—customized via the objective statement for the exact job he's looking to fill—it'll give him pause. He'll know you're not only interested but informed. Unlike many of the other applicants, you're not just casting your seed to the wind.

SNEAK IN THE GOOD STUFF

There are several different styles of resumes, each of which have strengths and shortcomings. For our purposes, we're going to discuss the most basic style—the chronological resume—simply because it is highly applicable for the right-out-of-college crowd and because most employers prefer it due to its simplicity.[2] A chronological resume lists your most recent employment and experiences first, then works backwards.

Following your objective, the rest of your resume must answer a simple question: Why you? What makes you the right person for the job? For most of us, it's a combination of experience, talents/skills, and education. The first two of these will be covered in the "Experience" section. This is a line-by-line history of your working life but it's packaged as advertising. Every word has meaning.

The "Experience" section is where you sell yourself. Don't think for a second you can get away with just listing your employer, position, and period of employment. Nothing's more boring, unless you were once a covert governmental assassin. (And still, I'd think long and hard about including that on your resume.) Instead, you need to punch up your employment list with details. Write what your job involved, what problems you solved, and what projects you handled. Summarize your responsibilities, while keeping in mind the qualities that will make you most attractive to the person reading them.

---

[2] Other useful styles include the *functional resume* (which focuses more on certain skill sets than detailed experience and is useful for those changing fields or with a wide variety of loosely-related experience) and the *curriculum vitae* (which is primarily used when entering a teaching or science position, wherein things like publications and honors are considered in detail). Obviously, a C.V. can be much longer than your average one- or two-pager.

Some examples:

- Project Coordinator, Midwest Printing, St. Louis, MO (1999-2001) Worked closely with dozens of customers in conjunction with sales representatives and prepress/printing staff to take projects from initial development stage to final printed and bound piece. Included conceptual brainstorming, production scheduling, and detailed proofreading for projects as diverse as product catalogs, regional direct mail campaigns and consumer magazines.

(Since "project coordinator" is a vague term, this description explains the particulars of your job—while also revealing your familiarity with large-scale projects, your organizational skills, your proofreading experience, and your frequent client contact. Each of these are attractive to any employer, regardless of the job.)

- Grant Writer, Bailey-Templeton University, Kansas City, MO (1998-1999) Duties included researching funding opportunities, writing grant applications and developing grant proposals for a mid-size private university. Worked closely with non-profit and charitable boards and planned/hosted a number of social fundraising events. Was successful in procuring nearly $3.5 million for capital improvements and scholarships over the course of 14 months.

(It's one thing to say you're a "grant writer." It's quite another to say you were instrumental in adding a cool three mil to the university's coffers. Even though that's not an abnormally large number for a well-established university, it sure seems impressive to the uninformed. Notice how this summary also touched on interpersonal, leadership, and organizational skills by way of the sentence on fundraising.)

The most important thing to remember is to use the descriptions to make your past jobs seem dynamic and productive. Perhaps your last work was as an administrative assistant, and your main responsibilities were faxing, photocopying, and answering phones. There's nothing wrong with that, but such a description is about as exciting as Stephen Wright on *Quaaludes*. Spice it up a little. How? First, think of a problem you helped solve. Then, depict that problem-solving process with impressive language.

Let's say you answered phones for a travel agency during the summers, and the boss was so impressed with your customer skills she asked you to develop some phone etiquette tips for the rest of the agency's employees to use. So instead of just saying you "answered phones," you can say you "helped research, devise, and implement new customer contact procedures." You may have held an entry-level position, but your job description paints you as more than that. You show yourself to be a problem-solver. That combination of critical thinking and assertiveness is something all employers are looking for.[3]

TAILOR YOUR EXPERIENCES

If you're applying for a job as research assistant for a medical supply company, there's no need to list your eighth grade paper route. Nor will the PR firm care that you were a lifeguard at the municipal pool during the summer after eleventh grade (though CPR certification might be worth mentioning).

The point is, you don't need to list every job you've ever had. The most recent two or three absolutely need to be there, but after that, list only the ones that are impressive or applicable. Ask yourself this question before summarizing your job duties: Was any aspect of this job relevant to the position currently being offered? If so, line-list the job, and show how it applies. Let's consider the municipal lifeguard applicant above. If she's applying for a job at a PR firm, the only reason she might want to list her summer lifeguarding experience is if part of that experience shared common ground with the desired position. Here's how that might look:

- Lifeguard, Clifton Marks Municipal Pool, St. Louis, MO (2000) Duties included enforcement of rules

---

[3] Please, please, please don't misunderstand here. I'm not saying to exaggerate or embellish your job experience. Lying on a resume is all kinds of wrong, and it'll eventually catch up to you. What I'm advising is to use active word choice and selective descriptions to make your duties—however conventional—seem impressive. And to further showcase your skills through the strategic use of detail.

and regulations and overseeing safety of all swim-
mers. In addition, worked closely with pool manager and local media in promoting "Fun in the Sun"
Summer Swim Camp for underprivileged youth—
wrote press releases, oversaw radio ad/PSA production and served as media contact.

Notice how she listed her broad-spectrum lifeguarding duties first,
then expanded on the more important advertising/marketing
aspects. A similar applicant looking for a nursing position after
graduation would want to focus on the medical aspects of her lifeguarding job:

* Lifeguard, Clifton Marks Municipal Pool, St. Louis,
  MO (2000) Duties included enforcement of rules
  and regulations and overseeing safety of all swim-
  mers. Received and have maintained lifeguard, first
  aid and CPR certifications. Assisted in demonstrat-
  ing first aid and CPR techniques for new employee
  orientation/training and attended additional Red
  Cross lifeguarding classes on Automated External
  Defibrillation (AED) and Oxygen Administration.

Whoever is reading your resume doesn't want to know every single thing you did in your job history. But they do want to know
about the things that might make you the perfect person for the
job they need to fill. Don't make them hunt for the pearls in your
resume or have to squeeze it out of you during an interview—
make those qualities the highlights.

MISCELLANEOUS TIPS

* Education. While all experts agree that listing the
  details of your education is necessary, there is some
  discussion as to whether it should appear before or
  after your work history. My advice would be to put
  it first if it meets one of the following criteria: 1) If
  your major was directly related to the position
  offered, or 2) If you attended a prestigious school
  (e.g. Stanford, Vanderbilt, Rice, Duke, or any Ivy
  League university). If it'll be an attention-grabber,
  put it first. If you graduated with an unrelated

degree from a ho-hum institution, put it toward the end of the resume. List the name of the school, your GPA (but only if it was a 3.4 or better), the degree(s) you received, and your major and minor. If you haven't yet graduated, include only the most up-to-date info.[4]

- Additional Information. This is the potpourri category, the place to include any information that doesn't readily fit into work history or education, but could be instrumental in selling yourself. For instance, you might want to list civic awards or charitable work. If you can speak another language or are a published author (weblogs don't count), list it here. List fluency or experience with relevant computer programs, or any leadership positions and civic organizations that might prove helpful. Almost anything is appropriate here as long as it pertains to the job being sought.[5]

- Format. Keep it simple. Keep it organized and aesthetically pleasing. Don't use goofy fonts. Do use bold fonts, a larger type size or capitalization to highlight the most important items, but keep whatever methods you use consistent throughout the resume. Absolute parallelism is necessary—if you put periods at the end of a date, then make sure you do so for every date. If your previous job title appears in bold, then make sure all titles are bold.

---

[4] If you attended college but never graduated, don't make a big deal of it. Instead, write something like "Attended Smith University, 1997-2000, majoring in French Literature with a minor in Business." The subtle difference between "attending" a university versus actually graduating from one may be lost on the speed-scanning employer.

[5] The "Additional Information" category is an ideal place to cover the touchy subject of race or ethnicity—if, that is, it can be used as an advantage. An often unmentioned aspect of the job application process is that employers are sometimes pressured to give special consideration to minority applicants. Unfortunately, employers can't always tell minority status from a name (and it's not exactly kosher to write "Steve Wilson, Black Man" at the top of your resume). Your best bet is to drop the hint by listing affiliations to which you belong: *Vice President, University of Notre Dame Black Students Association* (2000); or *Member, Society of Hispanic Professional Engineers (SHPE)*.

Print the resume on a nice white or cream paper stock, and don't be afraid of too much white space in the margins or between sections—this makes it easier to read.

- Usage. Since your resume needs to be action-oriented, leave out as many articles (a, an, the) and personal pronouns (I, me) as possible. Spell out any numbers up through ten, but use numerical form for eleven and above. Proofread. Then proofread again. Then have someone else proofread it. A mistake in a resume can cost you a job, so no typos.

- Contents. We've said it before, but it's worth mentioning again—your resume should be targeted toward the job for which you're applying. Put in the good stuff, and leave out the unimportant stuff. Some things should be included simply because they're expected. Therefore, every resume needs the following information: name, address, phone number (and e-mail address, if you have one), jobs held since beginning your full-time career (high school or summer jobs aren't necessary unless they specifically apply, as stated above), and educational info. Make sure the job and education lists are in reverse chronological order.

- Length. While you'll occasionally read that the basic chronological resume should always be one page, that's not life-or-death advice—it's definitely up for discussion. I'd rather present a two-page resume than trim something important from it just because I'm running out of room. As long as you can keep your reader's interest, a two- or even three-pager can be effective. The length doesn't matter—appropriate, enticing content does.

- Accuracy. Do not, do not, DO NOT put anything on your resume that you can't back up. It's important to impress your reader, but not important enough to allow you to risk your integrity on propaganda. Keep in mind, though, that it is okay to highlight your best features and downplay your deficiencies. This is precisely what happens in the world of advertising. Have you ever seen an ad for an SUV that mentioned its extremely poor gas mileage? No—instead you're told about its cargo capacity, safety features and powerful engine. In the same way, your resume is an ad for you. Don't stretch the truth, but don't be so honest that you call attention to a monstrous negative. Re-word that negative into a positive: inexperience becomes "fresh perspective," a lack of skills becomes "willing to learn," and so on.

- References. At the end of your resume, include the phrase "References available upon request." While it's important to supply applicable references to your would-be employers, it's not always smart to list them on the resume itself. By submitting them separately, you're free to tailor your reference list to the job being offered. You'll usually be asked for these following the first or second successful interview. Include three people with whom you've worked in the recent past—and, no, relatives don't count—who will be able to vouch for your personality, honesty, work habits, etc. While many may not, some employers actually contact your references, so make sure you get their permission before handing over their names. And the most important consideration of all: Make sure your references like you and will speak well of you. Good references can be the icing on the cake, but a bad reference can negate everything.

The resume-crafting process can be intimidating, particularly since it requires the ability to generate excitement through written description and explanation. I've seen a number of lifeless resumes that, had they been presented more efficiently, should have knocked the socks off a prospective employer, but you had to wade through acres of crap just to find the good stuff. Jennifer Aniston may be naturally beautiful, but drape her in a bulky jumpsuit and a ski mask, and that beauty's hard to see. She might as well be Barb, the cafeteria lady. Same goes for your resume—

make sure you sell yourself by emphasizing the jobs, skills, and experiences that matter. Put them front and center. Don't make your prospective employers search for them; they won't.

And don't be afraid to seek help in writing your resume. We've covered some basic principles and ideas, but there's more to it than the few pages you've just read. Plenty of resume-writing guides are available in print or online, as are countless formatting and design examples. Take advantage of these. Look at as many samples as you can to get a good idea of what works. Then, allow yourself enough time to do it right—a good resume can't be typed up in fifteen minutes.

So there you go. That's all there is to it—how to generate a good feeling, a solution to a problem, or some combination of both by way of a few words on a letter-sized sheet of paper. Easy, huh? Now, go find a job.

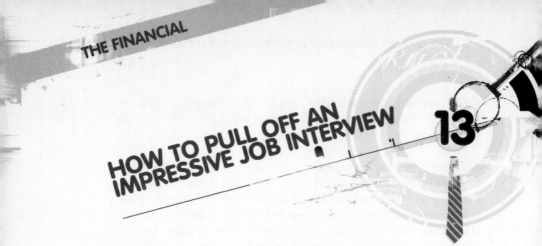

THE FINANCIAL

HOW TO PULL OFF AN IMPRESSIVE JOB INTERVIEW

13

All of us are intent on finding the perfect career. Ask a child what he or she wants to be when they grow up, and your answers will be as varied as hairstyles in San Francisco. A cowboy. A race car driver. An Olympic ice skater. A princess.

And that was just me.

Actually, when I was a kid, my dream was to be a paleontologist. Stop laughing. As soon as I could say it and much sooner than I could spell it, I had decided to be the kind of scientist who studies dinosaurs for a living, more than a decade before *Jurassic Park*. (Yes, I was that cool.) Like many childhood interests, the phase tapered off after a few years. But while it lasted, I was deeply into it. I distinctly remember correcting my kindergarten teacher during one of our first dinosaur lessons in school. She confused a Brontosaurus with the Brachiosaurus—an easy layperson's mistake, I know. I was not impressed with her knowledge. Nor, it seems, was she with mine.

As a kid, life spreads out before you like a desert highway. Pressures are non-existent, and options are plenty. Anything is possible. Life is good.

Then you graduate from college and smack head-on into the "Rest of Your Life" bus. You're expected to look for and get a job. Mom and Dad want you to start paying back your school loans. Your landlord wants his rent. Your dog wants to eat. And all you want is to be satisfied with a first job that doesn't suck, one that somehow—please, God, *somehow*—relates to your chosen field.

Only one cruel thing stands between you and occupational bliss: a garlicky, tattooed bouncer called the job interview. Nothing short of another season of *Survivor* strikes more fear into the hearts of post-college twentysomethings than the dreaded job interview. Why? Because it's intrinsically unknown. It's always different. It's tricky. It's the seed beneath a forest of self-doubt.

If things go too smoothly in a job interview, it's probably because you screwed up. If the experience was rocky, it's probably because you screwed up. If you called the interviewer "Mr. Lambada" when his name was actually Mr. Lentana, then you definitely screwed up. There are thousands of ways to muck up a job interview, from dressing wrongly to having a bad hair day to not knowing enough about the company beforehand.

That encouragement aside, there are also a number of things to keep in mind that can help you get off on the right foot. It's no day at the beach, but it's not as hard as you think. Here are a few tips to take the edge off the stress.

SHAKE LIKE A MAN (OR WOMAN)

A firm handshake is always, always appropriate for both male and female job applicants. It projects confidence. It creates a vital first impression. And for many interviewers, it can even hint at personality—according to a recent study by the University of Alabama, people with a strong handshake were found to be, as a rule, more confident than the fish-wristed.[1] The handshake is the first (and usually only) physical contact between you and your interviewer, so it needs to be done right.

Some handshake-related suggestions:

- Prevent your hands from becoming too sweaty by keeping them open—don't ball them into fists before the handshake. You might also keep a tissue in your pocket to surreptitiously wipe off excessive sweat. Most of all, don't worry too much about sweaty palms. We all have them, and if you think about it too much, you'll probably make it worse.

---

[1] William F. Chaplin, Ph.D., Jeffrey B. Phillips, Jonathan D. Brown, Nancy R. Clanton and Jennifer L. Stein, "Handshaking, Gender, Personality and First Impressions," *Journal of Personality and Social Psychology*, Vol. 79, No. 1.

(So, um ... good luck on that one.)

- Make eye contact during a handshake. The strongest handshake can turn sour if you refuse to look at your interviewer.
- Grip in moderation—not too firm, not too weak. As a general rule, assume the grip is going to be strong and match it.

DRESS APPROPRIATELY

Researchers at the University of Toledo have found that job applicants have less than thirty seconds to make their mark on interviewers.[2] First impressions are vital in the interview process, and—like it or not—most first impressions are gleaned from the way you look. Clothing is critical. You should dress professionally, conservatively, and as if you'd fit immediately into that workplace. Here's the rule: Find out how that company's best-dressed people clothe themselves, then try to look like them. Even if you're applying for a company that enjoys casual days, you need to dress up. In most cases, this will mean a suit for men (dark socks and shoes, white shirt, conservative tie). For women, dark suits also look professional, though they have more options (a colorful blouse is fine). Wear jewelry in moderation, plus comfortable heels and hose.

Additional tips:

- I know of one or two employers who say they always consider the watch of the person they're interviewing. That means no orange Scooby-Doo watches with Velcro™ straps—even if that's what you usually wear.
- Guys, make sure your shirt collar is crisply ironed and clean. Interviewers will spend 90 percent of their time focused on your face and neck. You don't want them staring at a rumpled, dirty collar.
- Ladies, keep your long hair pulled back so people can see your eyes and face. This will also prevent you from absent-mindedly playing with it when you get nervous.

---

[2] Jenni Laidman, "Making an Impression," *The Topeka Capital-Journal* (Posted June 25, 2001, at *cjonline.com/stories/062501/pro_impressions.shtml*).

SHOW CONFIDENCE

In a job interview, you will be advertising both yourself and your abilities. It's a balancing act—you don't want come across as too meek, nor do you want to annoy your interviewer with arrogance. Don't brag or boast too much, but don't sell yourself short by any means. Smile. Be attentive. Above all, make eye contact. Failure to do so may indicate shyness or even deceit among some people. Neither is ideal for landing a job.

The biggest challenge for many job applicants will be nervousness. Remember this: Everyone is nervous for interviews, and interviewers will expect that. But don't let your apprehension get the best of you. Among other things, an interviewer will be considering how you might handle the job based on how you handle the interview. If the tension makes your voice crack and your ears sweat, they'll likely notice.

On the other hand, if you prepare beforehand by studying your resume, mentally outlining some goals and objectives and anticipating a handful of questions, you're more likely to remain poised. Confidence in yourself will convince the interviewer you can handle the job. Just don't be overbearing or aggressive. An upfront, honest appraisal of your talents and abilities is expected and admired. A know-it-all is not.

KNOW THE COMPANY

If I want to work for XYZ International, it might be a good idea to find out exactly what kind of work XYZ International does. Not only is it common courtesy to know something about the company you're applying to work for, it's also common sense. You don't want to find out after the fact that the product you've been hired to market is illegal in thirty-seven states and is an embarrassment to your mother.

Yet surprisingly, failure to research the prospective company is one of the biggest mistakes job applicants make these days. Is it because we're lazy? Stupid? Apathetic? There are a number of explanations, but all that matters is whether you are prepared to answer this frequently asked question: "So tell me, what do you know about our company?"

In today's information-packed world, there is no reason not to know that answer. Get online. Look up the company's website or Google their name. Poke around. With a little searching, you can weed out the company's products and services, reputation, leadership, and possibly even its recent market performance. Upon answering the above question, don't rattle off so much information you seem obsessive. Offer just enough to let the interviewer know you've done your research. It'll earn you respect, and make you seem smart. That's good.

PRACTICE YOUR ANSWERS

Here's a confession: This entire chapter really isn't necessary, because the Internet is full of tips and techniques for almost any kind of job interview. That's why there's no reason for you to be caught off-guard by an interviewer's question. Certain questions are asked in almost every job interview, and you need to be prepared to answer them—don't count on being able to successfully ad-lib replies to questions like, "What is your greatest weakness?" or, "What challenging work issue have you recently faced, and how did you handle it?"

Almost any career resource center or job site will have a collection of potential questions to expect. Study them; don't take this part lightly. Have concrete examples ready in response to questions about your most significant personal and professional accomplishments. Be ready to describe both short- and long-term goals. Know your strengths and weaknesses. Above all, practice your answers.

A good idea is to have a friend ask questions, then honestly measure your response. While it may seem silly to do so, it's better to look like a dork to your roommate than to stumble in the interview, rambling about lost loves and mediocre athletic accomplishments after having being asked nothing more difficult than, "How would you describe yourself?"

ASK THE RIGHT QUESTIONS

At the end of an interview, you'll probably be asked whether you have any questions you'd like to ask. Your answer should always be "Yes." It's advisable to ask a question for no reason other than to continue to express interest in the company and position.

What do you ask? Start with the company itself. Ask how it has changed in the past three to five years. Ask how the current economy has altered the company's operations. Ask about the company's goals: Where does it expect to be within five years?

Or, ask for any position-related details that haven't yet been covered. What are its main objectives and responsibilities? What kinds of challenges or obstacles can you expect? Does the employer see the position's responsibilities changing in the near future? Should you be hired, what would be your first project or goal?

Asking attentive, knowledgeable questions at the end of the interview serves two purposes. It shows interviewers that you're thoughtful and focused, which helps them decide whether you're right for the job. Secondly, by clarifying the status of the company and details of the position, questions can help you decide whether the job's right for you.

As a corollary to this tip, don't ask the wrong questions. Don't ask about salary or compensation in the first interview (that's a more appropriate question for follow-up interviews). Don't ask when you'll get your first raise. Don't ask when you'll be promoted. Don't ask about the hours, how soon you can go on vacation, or whether you can have your own office. In short, don't give them any reason to dislike or distrust you in the first meeting.

At the end of the interview, express your genuine interest in the position. (A perceived lack of enthusiasm for the job can be a red flag for interviewers.) Tell them you want the job. Ask about the next step in the process. Thank him or her for their time, and leave on a positive, confident note with a handshake. Following the interview, be sure to send a thank-you note.

Remember—people who get jobs aren't necessarily the most accomplished or best-qualified applicants. In many cases, they were the ones who interviewed the best. Like any acting performance, preparation is critical. You have to know your character, your lines, your part. Interviewing by the seat of your pants only works if you're a butt model.

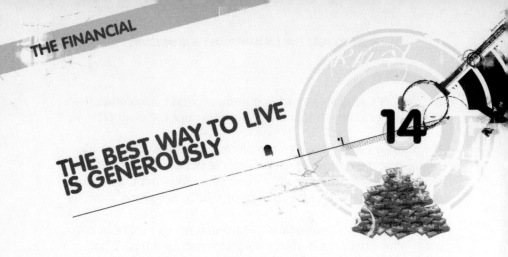

THE BEST WAY TO LIVE IS GENEROUSLY

14

"It is one of the most beautiful compensations of this life that you cannot sincerely try to help another without helping yourself."–Ralph Waldo Emerson

Consider the following statistics:

- Percentage of American teenage girls who report shopping as their favorite activity: 93 percent[1]
- Year in which the number of shopping centers in the U.S. (32,563) surpassed the number of high schools: 1987[2]
- Percentage of the world's population owning a car: 8 percent[3]
- Percentage of Americans who own a car: 89 percent[4]
- Number of second homes bought by Americans in 2000: 415,000 [5]
- Number of homeless Americans in 2000: around three million [6]

---

[1] Laurence Shames, *The Hunger for More* (New York: Times Books, 1989), 147.

[2] Alan Durning, "Asking How Much Is Enough," in Lester R. Brown et al, *State of the World 1991* (New York: W.W. Norton & Co., Inc., 1991), 163.

[3] Durning, 158.

[4] Jeremy Rifkin, Ed., *The Green Lifestyle Handbook* (New York: Henry Holt & Company, 1990), 33.

[5] Steve Bergsman, "Second-Home Market Is Poised to Rebound," *The Real Estate Journal* (Posted December 4, 2001 at *www.homes.wsj.com/buysell/second-homes/20011224-bergsman.html*).

[6] "Homelessness and Poverty in America," *National Law Center on Homelessness & Poverty* (Posted September 29, 2002 at *www.nlchp.org*). It's very hard to account for the number of homeless, since they drift in and out of public shelters from week to week and month to month. Most experts believe there are as many as 800,000 homeless on any given night, and more than three million over the course of a year.

Despite the last couple years of economic downturn, the United States and its citizens are living in a period of remarkable prosperity. It's been estimated that Americans own nearly 40 percent of the world's wealth while comprising only 2.5 percent of the world's population. That means if you have enough food to eat, enough clothes to keep you warm, a roof over your head, and a car to get you places, then you can count yourself wealthier than 85 percent of the rest of humanity. You may be a cash-deprived college student, a young professional just getting started, or a newlywed scraping by on a budget, but if you had the disposable income to buy this book (and thanks for that, by the way), then you're rich, comparatively speaking.

So ... the question is, do you feel guilty yet?

Should you feel guilty? Well, in a word: no. You can't help that you were born into Western culture and its abundance. There are plenty of other things to feel guilty about. Personally, I regret the time I stole a key blank from a K-Mart in New Mexico when I was eight years old. Just put it in my pocket, because I thought the shiny blue metallic finish on it was cool. Always felt bad about that. Wait, there's more: I regularly drive above the speed limit and roll through stop signs. I listen to pirated CDs. I once got free cable for a whole year until the cable company pulled the plug. I spend too much time doing what I want to do and too little time with my wife and kids.

And far too often, I find myself staring straight ahead at traffic lights, trying not to make eye contact with the grizzled bum on the corner. You've seen him: He's the one wearing three layers of clothing and six layers of grime, and he's holding the cardboard sign. The simple sign that reads, "Hungry. Please help."

That makes me feel worse than anything. Not because I have food, clothing, and shelter of my own. Not because I live a firmly middle-class lifestyle, which I've achieved by working hard and avoiding debt and living beneath my means. Not because, for all practical purposes, I was dealt a good hand from the beginning, having been born into a middle-class family during a prosperous period in the world's most prosperous country.

I don't feel guilty for having lucked into a comfortable life. But I do feel guilty when, for whatever reason, I refuse to share that comfort. Why? The answer is simple: Spider-Man, the movie. Remember the wisdom imparted to the reluctant Peter Parker by his uncle Ben? "With great power comes great responsibility." Or, in the words of a greater authority: "From everyone who has been given much, much will be demanded; and from the one who has been entrusted with much, much more will be asked."[7]

We've been given much. Compared to the rest of the world, we're the caretakers of great power, great wealth, great privilege, great opportunity. Maybe I'm more of a Pollyanna than I'd like to think, but I sincerely believe that, since we've been given so much, it's our responsibility to pass some of it around. I'm a believer in generosity. Not as an occasional virtue, but as a lifestyle. To paraphrase a minister friend of mine, "Make all you can, save all you can, share all you can." Or as a co-worker once put it, "The question isn't whether there's enough, but whether we're willing to share it."

So here's something you should know by now: Work hard. Make money, and don't be ashamed of it. But when the time comes, share it. Give. Practice charity. The best life is one of open-handed generosity. Here's why:

GENEROSITY COMBATS MATERIALISM

Consider another verse from the Bible, Matthew 19:24, paraphrased: "It is easier for a camel to go through the eye of a needle than for a rich man to enter the kingdom of God." As analogies go, this one is solidly Middle Eastern and, honestly, a little dated. Most of us don't have much contact with camels these days. Nor with needles, unless you run with druggies (or for that matter, seamstresses). So in case you can't relate, we'll wrap it up in more modern terminology: It's easier to drive a Hummer through a pierced ear than for a rich man to enter the kingdom of God.

Beyond the fanciful language, it's a documented fact that the wealthy give a much lower percentage of their income to charitable organizations than the poor. The reasons for this are varied. For one thing, while it's not so difficult to spare ten cents out of a

---

[7] Luke 14:48 (*New International Version*)

dollar, it's quite another story to surrender one hundred thousand dollars out of a million. Though the relative sacrifice may be greater, the dime is much easier on the psyche.

Wealth can also be distracting. Contrary to our what-if-I-won-the-lottery fantasies, wealth increases life's degree of difficulty—it makes love, friendship and relationships more challenging because it replaces financial burdens with a whole new set of interpersonal ones. Among them are insulation, distrust, stress—and the sudden appearance of long-forgotten relatives. Again, I'm not saying it's wrong to make money. But I do think it's wrong to make money and use it only to add feathers to your cap. There are a lot of needs in this world, but a second Lincoln Navigator is not one of them. The best way to fight our society's obsession with wealth and the toys it can buy us is to treat possessions like the fleeting extras they are. Materialism builds a shrine to the things we own. Generosity kicks the shrine over and gives away the parts.

Let's move from the theoretical level to the real world. Not the MTV program, though that would provide a fantastic example of materialism. Not to mention sexual irresponsibility. And the perils of drunkenness. And questionable hygiene, for that matter. No, I mean the real real world, the one with needy people, with poverty and famine. There are a number of practices that merge generosity with an anti-materialistic bent. Here are some examples:

1)   Giving away your money. This one's so obvious, I almost didn't include it. But here it is: From churches to children's charities to AIDS relief in Africa, nothing goes further than a good old American dollar. There are as many organizations out there as stars in the sky, but not all of them have the same twinkle. Before writing your check, do your homework. Find out how much of your donation actually goes to the cause. Some foundations give 100 percent to people in need. Others have heady operating costs, which they're required to divulge. Ask questions. Then, once you've found a charity with which you're comfortable, start sharing.

2) Giving away your extra stuff. All of us have closets packed with clothing we haven't worn since the last presidential administration. Perhaps we're waiting for the perfect occasion to wear that sequined halter top (I know I am). We're hoping our parachute pants will someday be stylish again. Or, more likely, we just grew bored with the perfectly fine wardrobe we had and bought something else. But if you don't wear it, and there's someone somewhere who would love it, why keep it? Yes, you could sell it on eBay, but that would be so predictable. Instead, give it away. Whether you have excess clothing, books, musical instruments, tools, or toys, chances are good that someone will be ecstatic to have it. If you can't part with something you no longer use, ask yourself why. If it has sentimental value, that's one thing. If it's because you paid a lot for it, then you best start slimming down your camel and searching for extra-large needles.

3) Sharing the stuff you keep. With the births of our two children, my wife and I experienced generosity on a firsthand basis. It began with the reality of a headfirst dive into the cash-burning world of baby supplies. As far as human lives go, there is no more expensive time than Year Zero through Year Two. Diapers, formula, baby food—all expensive, all useful for about five minutes. Same goes for the clothing. Baby clothes are sized according to month (zero to three, three to six, six to nine), so you're paying fifteen dollars for an outfit your child will wear maybe four times, best case scenario. Three if she spits up a lot. Twice if she has diaper issues. We were saved countless times by our family and friends, who willingly loaned us boxes full of baby clothing. They had the right idea: Is it better for this outfit to hang in a closet somewhere or to be put to use on a child? The same applies to maternity clothing, old computer systems, tools, even vehicles. Make your possessions available to others, and they'll naturally become less important to you (especially when, as it often happens, you don't get them back).

GENEROSITY EXTENDS YOUR INFLUENCE

As soon as her three kids entered elementary school, my paternal grandmother, Mary Boyett (we call her Memaw), went to work. She took a job at a local bank, first as a teller and secretary, then later as an attendant to the bank's mainframe computer system, implemented in the early seventies. She and my grandfather lived frugally, saving as much as they could. Each of them took large portions of their wages in company stock, hoping one day to better the lives of their children and grandchildren. They've been successful.

My brother, sister, three cousins and I have all benefited from what we fondly call the "Memaw Scholarship." It originated with the stock she purchased from her employer. Over the past two decades, that bank has been sold at least five different times, and with each new purchase, her stock has bumped or split. She has periodically withdrawn from it to help send her grandkids to college, paying for books, tuition, and room and board—even making loans to us for our first cars. Now that we've moved out of the dorms and into the working world, she's determined to use her savings to help us each make decent down payments on our first homes. That's been her plan all along. "What would I do with it?" she always asks us. "Go to Vegas?" She's happy to spend each day quilting. My grandfather is happy listening to Paul Harvey, watching PBS, or dozing in his recliner. And they're happiest when they see their grandchildren succeed.

That's generosity, and we'd all do a lot worse than to follow their example. My grandparents have led a simple life. They live in a modest home, drive practical cars, and attend a small church. She was a mom and worked at a bank, he a World War II veteran and worked at a refinery. Yet portraits of their generosity are painted daily by the lives they helped shape—among them, an award-winning poet, two successful businessmen, a writer and musician, a beloved teacher, and a doting father of twins. A half-dozen great-grandkids (with more on the way) living happy lives in nice homes built on down payments bolstered by occupations achieved by education gained through the Memaw Scholarship. All my grandparents wanted to do was to help us out, but they ended up making us who we are.

A lifestyle of giving meets immediate needs, but it also lays a foundation for the future. And by way of that foundation, one's life grows exponentially, extending into future generations. Put simply, sharing makes you bigger than you are. My grandparents are nearing eighty. They may not be around a whole lot longer, but their legacy will.

GENEROSITY CHALLENGES SELFISHNESS

I'm not going to resort to the usual clichés, nor will I spoon-feed you with any more "here's why we're so self-centered" statistics. I'm self-involved, you're self-involved, and both of us know it (sheesh—how many times, by the way, have I used the words I, me or my in this chapter?). We're selfish people by nature, turtles who, at the merest hint of discomfort or danger, retreat into our shells. We close our eyes, hug ourselves tight, and refuse to let anything else in.

There's nothing explicitly wrong with that. As Ayn Rand was fond of telling us, being concerned with your own interests is the only way to protect your well-being. That kind of practical self-centeredness is necessary in order to live a fulfilling, productive life. But when such a mindset begins to exalt your own well-being at the expense of others, then it turns into the bad kind of selfishness, the kind that takes advantage of people—or completely ignores them—to satisfy personal needs. Grabbing an umbrella when it begins to rain? That's an acceptable self-centeredness. But grabbing an umbrella out of an old lady's hand? That's the bad kind.

Our problem is the ease by which we can slide from Point A (self-protection) to Point B (self-protection at poor old Ethel's expense). Like trying to brake on an icy road, our early attempts to stop are hindered by momentum.

Here's another analogy, from the story-rich world of Zen: The Japanese master Nan-in once met with a university professor who came to inquire about Zen. Nan-in, always a gracious host, served tea to his visitor. He poured until the professor's cup was full, but didn't stop there. He kept pouring and pouring. The hot tea went everywhere, sloshing over the sides and onto the table. The professor watched in disbelief until he couldn't help himself. "That's enough!" he said. "The cup is full. No more will go in." Nan-in smiled and said, "You are the same. Like this cup, you are full of opinions and speculations. How can I show you Zen unless you first empty your cup?"[8]

Day in and day out, our lives are being filled with the stuff of self. We work for personal fulfillment; we work to make money. The fulfillment gives our lives meaning; the money supports our lifestyles. We make decisions based on our personal goals. We pursue leisure to provide balance. We rest in order to recharge. All of these are necessary, but all focus inward. By the simple nature of living, we're constantly filling our cups with self. Again, not wrong—just the way we're made. But the more self we put in, the less room there is for the truly important things. These are the virtues of selflessness—love, compassion, understanding—and we must make room for them. Generosity of time, money, and possessions is a way of emptying our cup, of making space. The more we pour out, the more life will be able to pour back in.

Two final thoughts: First, we've been thinking primarily about generosity as it relates to possessions and money, but don't forget that one of the most valuable commodities in today's society is time. Volunteerism, simply, is generosity as it pertains to time. While our parents' generation may have been more likely to support a charitable cause or organization with their checkbook, members of our generation seem to be more willing to give hours of our time. Volunteerism is just as valid a form of giving—it, too, is a way to "empty the cup." If you can't afford to help financially, help in other ways. Doesn't matter how, as long as you help.

Second, recognize that not all charitable opportunities are equal. Particularly scurrilous are the ones that bring glory to the giver, the ones that offer multiple opportunities to let the right hand know exactly what the left hand is doing. When Paul McCartney wed Heather Mills in an elaborate $3 million ceremony last summer, the couple achieved major press coverage out of their plan to sell photos of their nuptials to news agencies for nearly $1,500 a pop. The proceeds were donated to Heather's landmine charity.[9]

---

[8] Paul Reps and Nyogen Senzaki, *Zen Flesh, Zen Bones* (Boston: Tuttle, 1998), 19.
[9] "McCartney Ties Knot at Rock 'n' Roll Wedding," CNN.com (Posted June 13, 2002, at *www.cnn.com/2002/SHOWBIZ/Music/06/11/mccartney.wedday*).

Would it have been too much to ask for the McCartneys to just have a less expensive ceremony? To donate a chunk of money on their own instead of going through the elaborate self-puffery of the wedding photo gimmick? As they say, generosity that sticks to your fingers is no generosity at all.

True, selfless giving, though, remains one of our loftiest aims. It makes us richer than money or possessions ever could. Like any habit, it needs to be cultivated, but the yield is remarkable. Don't wait until the cup is so full your life starts sloshing onto the floor. Start the habit of sharing now, whether it's your time, your money or your stuff. You won't regret it.

THE PRACTICAL

HOW TO CHANGE A FLAT TIRE

15

At the end of 1995, during the Christmas holidays, a stretch limousine pulls over to the side of a busy New Jersey highway. Flat tire. An inexperienced chauffeur gets out to change the flat, but struggles with the spare, the jack, and the bulky vehicle. The limo's passengers begin to grow impatient. A passing motorist, perhaps out of a sense of seasonal goodwill, decides to stop and ask if the driver needs any assistance. Fearing for his job, the chauffeur accepts immediately. The kindly Samaritan helps change the tire without incident, and the driver thanks him. Just before the vehicle cruises away, one of the darkly tinted windows rolls down. A man calls out from inside. "Hey," the voice says, "Thanks for your help."

The kind motorist approaches the window, and looks inside: Donald Trump. Next to him is current wife Marla Maples. "What can I do to repay you?" Trump asks. The guy shrugs. "Just send my wife a big bouquet of flowers," he says. "She'd be thrilled to get flowers from a celebrity." He gives the billionaire his name, his wife's name, and their address. They part ways.

Two weeks later, a monstrous bouquet of orchids arrives at the Samaritan's home. Attached is a card. It reads, simply: "Thanks so much for your help. We paid off your home mortgage—Marla and Donald."

Cue dramatic music.

First, a disclaimer: This really didn't happen. It's an urban legend, and precisely the kind of unexpected windfall/good Samaritan/generous celebrity story that makes the rounds because people love to hear about good deeds being returned.

Similar tales are attributed to Perry Como, Mrs. Nat King Cole, and even Ivana Trump.[1]

But just because it didn't really happen doesn't mean we can't learn something from it, right? After all, we've all learned a good lesson or two from Aesop's fables, Mother Goose, and *Family Ties*. Why not this story? I think its lesson is obvious: Learn to change a flat tire, and you will be handsomely rewarded by a hideously wealthy and well-known real estate magnate with creepy hair.

Let's put mythmaking aside for a moment and get to the point. If you drive at all, you need to know how to change a flat tire. Otherwise, you'll find yourself stuck by the side of the road, either waiting for AAA to arrive or worrying that some deranged scar-face with a hook for a hand will show offering to help (and to top it off, he'll probably expect you to pay off his mortgage, too). That said, now's as good a time to learn as any. Here are your instructions, step-by-step:

1) PLAN AHEAD.

Before you take off for any sort of lengthy drive, you should always check for a couple of tire-related items. First, make sure you have a spare. In cars, you'll generally find the spare under the floor of the trunk. Most trucks and SUVs will stow the spare beneath the chassis at the rear. Whether it's a full-sized spare or one of those temporary high-pressure "self-destruct-after-fifty-miles" ones, make sure the tire is both accessible and fully inflated.

Next, confirm the location of both the jack and a tire tool (usually found in the same place as the spare). Often, the tire tool that comes with the car is small and wussy and hard to manage. (Then again, I've also been described that way. Sigh.) A good idea is to go to an auto supply store and procure yourself a brawny, burly jack—one of those drop-forged cross-shaped ones. Not only are

---

[1] Additional examples of this and related legends can be found at *www.snopes.com*, home of the remarkably useful Urban Legends Reference Pages, created and collected by Barbara and David P. Mikkelson. For more on urban myths and legends, be sure to read the chapter in this book titled, appropriately, "Beware the Urban Legend."

they comforting in their symbolism, but they give you much better leverage on sticky lug nuts. More on that later.

2) PULL OVER SAFELY.

When a tire gets punctured by road debris or suddenly blows out while you're driving, you'll know it—the way your car handles will noticeably diminish. You'll probably experience a little unsteadiness at the steering wheel or a pulling to one side. Don't panic, and don't overcorrect. Instead, slowly apply pressure to the brake while steering to the side of the road.

At this point, you'll need to find a good place to jack up the car. It needs to be as far away from traffic as possible, especially at night, when oncoming cars will have a difficult time seeing you crouched at the side of the road. It also needs to be a firm, level surface—you don't want to use a jack on a hill or incline. Remember Jack and Jill ... up a hill ... breaking his crown? That's where the nursery rhyme originated—a bad tire-changing experience.

Anyway, stop at the first good spot you find along a straight section of road (curves are dangerous places to stop). If you have to, it's okay to drive a short distance on a flat tire, as long as you do it very slowly, realizing that the further you drive, the greater the risk of damaging the tire or the wheel itself. When you come to a stop, shift the car into park (reverse for a manual transmission) and apply the parking brake. Turn on your emergency flashers. If it's dark, you might also want to turn on one of the vehicle's interior lights to help you see more clearly.

3) SPARE. JACK. WHEEL COVERS.

Find your spare tire, jack, and lug wrench, and arrange them within reach. Usually, the jack handle will double as the lug wrench, but if you're using a true lug remover (the testosterone-satisfying cross-shaped one), that won't matter.

There are several types of jacks. Yours may be a bumper jack that fits into a slot beneath the bumper. Others are screw-type scissors jacks that should be placed under the vehicle axle or suspension. Your owner's manual will contain instructions for operating the jack. Often, a decal near the spare tire will have the same info.

(If you can't figure out how to use the jack, you'll need to locate an incredibly strong guy who can lift up more than one thousand pounds and hold it steadily for, say, ten minutes. If such a person is unavailable—just your luck, right?—call roadside assistance. Jacking up a car is reasonably safe, but can be tricky. If you aren't certain how it's supposed to work, don't risk it. Get help.)

The next step is to get to the lug nuts by removing the wheel cover or hubcap. These will need to be pried loose using the flat end of the lug wrench or jack handle. Once the hubcap comes off, don't let it roll away. That can be embarrassing.

4) LOOSEN THE LUG NUTS.

Before jacking up the car, you'll need to first begin loosening the lug nuts. Otherwise, the wheel will just spin on you (another embarrassment just waiting to happen.) Find the end of the wrench that fits and place it snugly over any of the lug nuts. Turn counter-clockwise, using the "crossbar" of the wrench to gain leverage. This can be awkward, as lug nuts often are so tight they don't budge on the first attempt. Don't worry, though—we're prepared for this scenario. Here's what you should do: Steady the wrench with one hand, and step down hard on the other end. If that doesn't work, steady yourself on the car and climb up onto the wrench. Put your full weight on the left-hand side of the wrench (yet another reason to get the big cross-wrench—this is much more difficult with the jack-handle version) and give it a good bounce.

Once you get the nut going, loosen it one or two full turns while the wheel is still on the ground. It should be loose enough that you can turn it the rest of the way by hand, which you'll do after the car is jacked up. Lather, rinse, repeat.

5) MEET JACK.

To remove the wheel, you'll need at least a half-inch or so of ground clearance. This, of course, is where the jack comes in handy. First, insert the handle into the socket on the jack. To begin lifting the vehicle, you'll either turn the handle or pump it like scissors (again, check your owner's manual to see what type of jack you have). Raise the jack until it barely touches the car, then position it according to the directions in your manual. Each car has a certain place near each wheel designed for safe jack contact. It's usually less than a foot behind the front tire or a foot ahead of the back tire.

Once your jack is positioned correctly, give it a few good cranks. Lift the vehicle so that the tire has enough room to spin and then lift it a little more. After all, you'll need to fit a full-capacity inflated tire in its place. For good measure, crank the jack a couple more times.

6) OFF WITH THE OLD, ON WITH THE NEW.

Hopefully, the lug nuts are still on the old wheel (honestly, it's killing me not to make some sort of testicular joke here). Turn them by hand until they completely loosen, and remove them. Don't misplace them—a good idea is to rest them in the basin of the nearby hubcap.

If you have gloves, this would be a good time to put them on, as tires can be filthy. Grab the old wheel on either side and pull it straight off. At this point, extra cautious tire-changers will sometimes place the old, flat tire and wheel under the side of the car. That way, should the jack fail, the car won't fall to the ground, damaging its underside and squashing you like an ant on the street during a steamroller parade.

Moving on. At any rate, put the old tire aside. Install the new one by lining up the spare's center holes with the threaded shafts on the wheel base. Depending on how high you've jacked the car, you may need to raise it another notch or two to have room for the new tire. Tighten the lug nuts as much as possible—but not all the way—while the wheel is raised off the ground. Then lower the jack.

Now it's time to tighten the nuts the rest of the way. To make sure the wheel is securely balanced, work in a star-shaped pattern. Give a full turn to the topmost nut. Skip the next one, then give another full turn to next lug nut. Carry on in this manner over three or four tightening stages, until every nut is tight and flush against the wheel.

7) ON THE ROAD AGAIN.

Lower the jack according to the instructions in your owner's manual. Once the weight is removed, the jack will likely topple over. Once this occurs, keep bringing it down until the jack is fully closed. Then, all that's left is to clean up after yourself. Put the wheel cover or hubcap back on. Stow the damaged tire, jack, and tire tool back in your vehicle. Wipe your brow, pat yourself on the back, and carefully ease into traffic.

Note: If you replaced your flat tire with a small, temporary, space-saver tire, please remember that it's only intended to allow you to drive to the nearest service station. It's not designed to take you a long distance, nor is it designed to go in excess of 50 mph. Drive carefully to the next facility, and have your flat repaired by professionals. They'll fix it and put the repaired or new tire on for you.

And should they get confused at any point during the tire-changing process, you'll be on hand to offer expert advice—or to pay off their home mortgages. One or the other. Just use your best judgment.

HOW TO SPEAK GOOD ... ER, WELL

16

In the fourth grade, I had a teacher named Mrs. McCartor. She was old and crotchety, and wore lime-green polyester granny dresses with matching shoes. High-heeled platform shoes. While her appearance might have made her unintentionally stylish a couple of years ago, she was decidedly uncool in 1985. Of course, as a twelve-year-old boy who wore sweat pants seven days a week, I was decidedly uncool myself.

But I digress.

Mrs. McCartor had a thing for proper grammar, and she drilled us relentlessly. We diagrammed sentences, identified subjects and predicates, and learned the difference between "lay" and "lie." We lived in constant fear of failure, having heard from older, more experienced fifth-graders of the dreaded "McCartor Milkshake"—a grim humiliation applied to the skinny shoulders of those students who overlooked the rules of proper grammar. I was never on the receiving end of one of those milkshakes, nor do I remember actually seeing one being inflicted. But I imagined it, and worried about it, and I fearfully made a point to learn the rules of proper grammar. So did everyone else.

Then, once school was out and the milkshake threats had melted into the summer heat, we completely forgot those rules. And I mean completely. Eight years later, Mrs. McCartor called me up on a Monday morning in June. It was the week following my high school graduation. She had seen my name in the paper, where the local graduates were listed, and remembered me. I believe we had a pleasant, albeit brief, how's-life-been conversation. She asked me how I'd enjoyed high school, how my family was doing, what were my plans for college.

At least I think she asked those things, but I'm basing that mostly on conjecture, because—just between you and me—I remember very little of the actual conversation. I spent the whole time sweating over the swirl of competing sentences in my head: I'm going to lie down. I'm going to lay down. Lie down. Lay down.

Dear God. Which sentence was correct? I was certain she was going to ask, and my sad little pretense of an education was going to become public knowledge. Mrs. McCartor was going to kill me.

She didn't, and the sickening glop in the pit of my stomach soon disappeared. I went on to complete my college education as an English major, making sure I learned once and for all the truth behind the two most feared words in the English language: lay and lie.

You, too, should know the difference, and here's why: People judge you on the way you talk. They judge your vocabulary, your sentence structure, even your accent. True, most people won't detect run-of-the-mill grammar gaffes. But if you happen to inter-view with a former English teacher, or anyone else for whom proper speaking is a virtue, you don't want to immediately call attention to your lack of linguistic polish.

There's a saying in the British Isles: "Speak one way, and you'll be running the country. Speak another way, and you'll be cleaning it." In that society, speech patterns and usage are hugely impor-tant. They call attention to everything from education level to birthplace to social standing. Things aren't so cut-and-dried in the U.S. In fact, our forty-third President has been known to publicly mangle a sentence or two. But the point is, there is a right and wrong way to speak. Even if no one else will judge you for saying something like, "I axed him at the lie-berry where them books were at," please be certain the Mrs. McCartors of the world will.

So pay attention. Here's something you should know by now: It's important to be able to speak articulately, a skill which requires a basic adherence to the rules of grammar. Unfortunately, grammar is boring, and most of us tuned it out in ninth grade. We didn't care then, nor do we care now. Some of you have stopped reading already.

For those of you who are still around, I've identified two of our most confused grammar scenarios—"lay" versus "lie" and "good" versus "well"—and will hereby attempt to shed light on the differences between them with style, clarity, and delightful humor. Or, at the least, muddled rambling and sarcasm. Let's get started.

LAY VS. LIE

In its most basic form, the rule is this: "Lie" is an intransitive verb, meaning it does not take a direct object—it's something you do to yourself. Therefore, you're going to lie down.

> *I have eaten a bad taco, so I think I should* lie *down.*

It follows that "lay" is a transitive verb—it's something you do to someone or something else. As a result, "lay" is followed by a direct object.

> *Because the bad taco tastes like feet,*
> *you should* lay *it down and walk away.* (object: it)
> *I'm gonna* lay *down my burdens,*
> *down by the riverside.* (object: burdens)

Easy, right? Yes, it might seem so, until you consider the past tense, which is where most of us get screwed. This is where the McCartor Milkshake lulls us into complacency, waiting to reach out and grab us with polyester-wrapped arms of fury once the mistake is made. Seriously, it does get confusing here. The past tense of "lie"? You got it: "lay."

> *I* lie *down today. Yesterday, because of the taco, I* lay *down.*

The past tense of "lay"—the transitive verb, the one you do to something else—is "laid":

> *I* lay *down the bad taco today. Yesterday, I* laid *it down.*

And just for kicks, let's look at the past participles. First, the past participle conjugation of the verb "lie" is "lain":

> *By this time tomorrow, I will have* lain *down*
> *for twenty-four hours, because of that stupid taco.*

The past participle conjugation of "lay" is "laid":

> *By next Tuesday, he will have* laid *down thirty bad tacos in a seven-day period, which must be some kind of record.*

It's all becoming so clear, now, right? Let's continue.

GOOD VS. WELL

Scenario: You meet an old friend from high school. He smiles, sizes you up, wonders whether he's more successful than you, calculates which one of you has put on more weight (note to self: lay off the tacos), then asks, "How've you been doing?"

Most common response? "I'm doing good."

Nope. Wrong answer. You're not doing good—you're doing well. Confusing the two is so prevalent in our society that hardly anybody notices it anymore. In fact, some dictionaries have begun classifying the mistake as informal usage. But we know better than to accept that, because there is something to be said for being an above average speaker of English.

"Good" is an adjective. It modifies nouns and pronouns:

> *Your tattooist did a good job on that winged demon.*
> ("Good" modifies "job.")

> *You got a winged demon tattoo? Ooooh ... that's not good.*
> ("Good" modifies "tattoo.")

"Well," on the other hand, is an adverb. It's used to answer the question "How?" as a modifier of verbs, adjectives, and other adverbs:

> *How'd Mom do during the tattooing process? She did well.*
> ("Well" modifies the verb "did.")

> *I'll say this for your Mom—she wears a winged demon tattoo well.*
> ("Well" modifies "wears.")

117

So, athletes don't "play good," and singers don't "sing good." They play well and sing well. That's easy enough. The trouble starts when enter the realm of linking verbs and subject complements, especially when we talk about how we feel, or how we are. "Feel," like forms of "to be," is a linking verb. It connects the subject with a subject complement. For instance, in the sentence "You are dumb," the subject (you) is linked to the complement (dumb) by the linking verb (are).

Unfortunately, "good" and "well" are both often used as subject complements. Therefore, "I am good" is just as correct as "I am well." Same goes for "I feel good" and "I feel well." Hmm.

Here's the difference. In a subject complement situation, "well" should refer to health or the body:

I don't feel well in my stomach,
especially after seeing that tattoo.
I am well, except for this debilitating nausea.

Meanwhile, "good" is used to describe your mental/emotional state or your character:

I thought I'd feel good after seeing
my new forehead tattoo, but I was wrong.
Speaking of forehead tattoos,
Charles Manson is a bad person, but I am good.

To summarize: Good speakers of English speak well, and feel good about doing so. Though the copious amounts of grammar in this chapter may have given you a headache—keeping you from feeling well—it was presented well enough to give you a good grasp of the difference between "good" and "well."

And that's all well and good.

Of course, I know the real question you're asking, despite my elo-quent defense of proper speaking at the beginning of the lesson: Who the heck cares? And honestly, that's a valid point. Because unless you're one of those strict but well-meaning grammar zealots, standing fast behind good sentence construction like it was the final stronghold between doilied tea parties and anarchic desolation, "lay" versus "lie" doesn't matter that much in the grand scheme of things. It ranks right up there with being able to name the ten highest mountains in the world or the shortest and tallest U.S. presidents.[1] Let's all admit it—it just feels more natural to say "I'm gonna go lay down," or, "We're doing good," doesn't it? Even though they're technically wrong, the incorrect usage is so prevalent in our society it might as well be right.

Language is funny that way; it is entirely fluid. What's proper today might fall out of favor tomorrow, and vice versa. Consider *The Flintstones*, who, upon their debut in 1960, promised viewers "a gay old time" right there in the theme song. (Not that there's anything wrong with that.)

Or take the cursive capital "Q," which confused us all when we learned the basics of penmanship. Wasn't that just a fancy number two? Who made that up? Turns out we weren't alone. The cursive "Q" has all but fallen out of proper penmanship. No one uses it anymore. This point has more to do with writing systems than language, but the reality is this: On occasion, the idea of propriety gives way to common usage. Most people don't know that the intransitive "lay down" is just plain wrong. More importantly, they just don't care. "Lay" and "lie" have, therefore, become virtually interchangeable, as have "good" and "well."

So lay down if you want, particularly if you don't feel good after a bad taco encounter. But while you are doing so, remember that the best way to get people to take you seriously and respect you is to sound intelligent when you speak to them. First impressions are important. Bad first impressions can be deadly. Don't fall prey to one just because you think grammar and vocabulary are for geeks. They are, of course, but in today's world, geeks are running the show.

Postscript: Mrs. McCartor, if you're still alive and happen to read this, I don't mean to make you sound all that mean and scary.

---

[1] In order: Everest, K-2, Kangchenjunga, Lhotse, Makalu, Cho Oyu, Dhaulagiri, Manaslu, Nanga Parbat, and Annapurna, all of which are in the Himalayas. Abraham Lincoln was the tallest president, at six foot, four inches. James Madison was the shortest at five foot, four inches. And he weighed less than one hundred pounds, so I could have taken him.

Certainly, you were mean and scary back when I was twelve, but I was shorter then, and always believed everything the big kids said. When you called after I graduated? That was nice of you. You seemed genuinely proud. So please forgive me for making fun of your polyester, and for forgetting most of what you taught me, and also for exploiting you just now in the guise of creative concept introduction. My bad.

17 HOW TO BUY GROCERIES

The supermarket can be a dangerous place. In February of 2002 at the Market Basket in Lowell, Massachusetts, shopper Karen Morgan surreptitiously counted the number of groceries brought into the twelve-items-or-less express checkout line by the customer ahead of her, Alice Tooks. The thirty-eight-year-old Morgan counted no less than thirteen items in Took's basket, one too many. She was understandably upset. Her only recourse to this injustice—really, it makes perfect sense—was ruthless violence.

While still inside the store, Morgan began cursing at the fifty-one-year-old Tooks, berating her for her inability to count among other, more colorful shortcomings. Tooks eventually left the store and began walking home, but that wasn't the end of it. Morgan jumped in her car, driving off after the brazen express lane perp. She pulled up beside her, stepped out of the car and proceeded to beat her into the ground. She yanked the victim's hair and kneed her in the gut, hard enough to knock her down. Then, while Tooks was writhing on the asphalt, Morgan seized the opportunity to go Landon Donovan on her head. Shoe meet scalp. Scalp met pavement. Despite the trauma, the victim kept her wits long enough to memorize the car's license plate as Karen Morgan drove off.

The plate was subsequently traced to Morgan. She was arrested an hour later at her home—where she was found hiding in a closet—and charged with assault and battery with a deadly weapon (her foot). She faces up to ten years in prison if convicted.[1]

So let that be a lesson to you, fellow shoppers: A trip to the grocery store is not to be taken lightly. Nor, apparently, are express

---

[1] Lisa Redmond, "Express Line Rage Suspect Held on $5G Bail," *The Lowell Sun*: February 26, 2002.

lane infractions, but that's another chapter—we're here to talk about buying groceries. How to do it right (and violence-free) is one of the things you should know by now.

THE BASICS

My maternal grandfather, a man with the inventive name of John E. Brown, is known by most as Brownie. He lives in the Dallas/Ft. Worth Metroplex, and has made grocery shopping an art form. Brownie retired twenty years ago as warehouse manager for a large regional grocery chain, but still maintains a fondness for the industry—so much so that today, aside from golf, grocery shopping is his hobby. He doesn't just go to the grocery store; he goes to grocery stores. Give him a list, and he'll concoct a strategy. Brownie knows which of the five nearest supermarkets have the freshest grapes. Or the ripest tomatoes. Or the best deals on canned corn. Just try to get him to buy romaine lettuce at the market across the street—he won't even think of it, not when the regional chain a mile away has a far superior product and price. Not to mention double coupons on Wednesdays. For my grandfather, grocery shopping is a serious pursuit, and not for the faint of spirit. Here, then, are his tips for a successful trip to the supermarket:

1) Express lane signage is to be read and obeyed. I think this goes without saying.

2) Know what items you need before you go. If you shop once a week, plan your week's menu prior to the trip. Peruse the pantry to see if anything's running low. You don't want to buy something you already have, nor do you want to come home only to find out you're low on flour. Or hominy. Or whatever. Make a list; check it twice.

3) Calculate how much you'll need. Buying in bulk saves money, but it's no good to do so if half the product goes to waste or gets thrown away once you've grown tired of it. Don't buy the biggest bunch of grapes or jumbo-sized boxes of Chocolate Frosted Sugar Bombs if you won't finish them off. Large quantities are only economical once they're gone.

4) Eat before you shop. Supermarkets smell, look, and feel good. The produce glistens, the bread is piping hot, and the aroma in the coffee aisle is enough to give you jitters by itself. If you enter this environment on an empty stomach, you'll fall prey to impulse buys and a grocery bill that expands as fast as your waistline. Eat first and you'll have a much easier time sticking to your list.

5) Be adventurous. Did you know that grocery stores' most profitable (read: expensive) products are usually at eye level? That's because marketing research indicates you're more likely to buy the first product you see. The best values require bending and stretching, and most often are the "house" brands— the less-expensive, non-national products. Fact is, they're pretty much the same as the big brands (consistent nutritional quality is required), but without the fancy packaging and expensive marketing costs. Generics have come a long way from the black-and-white label stigma of twenty years ago. Don't be a corporate tool: Take a chance on a generic.

6) Be aware. The eye-level thing isn't the only trick grocery stores have behind their aprons. There's a reason you have to walk all the way to the back of the store—past aisle upon aisle of cookies and cereal—just to grab a gallon of milk. And those end-of-the-aisle displays that make it look like a product is on sale? Sometimes there's no sale at all. But we're suckers for the feeling of accomplishment we get when we think we've discovered a (supposedly) good deal, and we'll buy something we don't need just to pat ourselves on the back. So we end up with two bags of chips and an armful of soft drinks that weren't on our list—not to mention the whipped cream and strawberries that were conveniently placed near the pound cake. No, we weren't planning to make strawberry shortcake, but it suddenly seemed like such a good idea ...

7)   Talk to the employees. They can give you an idea of when fruit, vegetable, and dairy shipments come in, whether it's day-to-day or hour-by-hour. By being aware of their schedule, you can plan accordingly and come home with fresher, longer-lasting groceries.

8)   Scan the scanner. Even in today's wired world of grocery shopping, mistakes can be made in the checkout process, particularly when it comes to sale items. Keep your eyes on the display. It's better to catch an error as it occurs than to come back and quibble over a twenty-cent difference in the price of your sliced olives. If there's one thing you don't want to be known for, it's for being all weird about your olives.

THE SPECIFICS: FRUITS

Question: What good is an efficient, knowledgeable trip to the store if you don't come home with decent product? Answer: about as good as coming home from the dentist with Oreos® in your teeth.

No, I'm not sure what that's supposed to mean, either.

It's easy to buy a can of sliced peaches or green beans, because someone else does the choosing for you. But everyone knows the best value and nutrition can be found in fresh produce, so top shoppers avoid canned foods. It takes a little experience, though, to come home with a basket full of juicy goodness. Here are some specific things to know about the most popular produce:

•   *Apples*. Look for a deep, uniform color with few blemishes, soft spots, or indentions. For a little snacking variety, try Gala or Braeburn apples instead of the usual (but so overexposed) Red Delicious or Granny Smith apples. Just a tip.

•   *Bananas*. I like them tinged with green on the ends; they're sweeter that way. Look for a firm, uniform color, and don't be afraid to buy them a little green—they'll ripen at home. Avoid the soft or spotted.

- *Berries*. Except for blueberries, most berries are very perishable. When buying blackberries, raspberries, or boysenberries, look for firm, solid, plump product. Avoid berries that are starting to soften or "juice" or look moldy. You'll need to use them right after they've been washed.

- *Cantaloupe*. To check for ripeness, gently press the large indentation on the end of the melon. It should give slightly. Then give it a sniff: A ripe melon will have a sweet, fragrant aroma.

- *Grapes*. Look for bunches that are firm and clustered tightly to the stems. Seedless are best. Store grapes uncovered in your fridge for optimum crispness.

- *Lemons and limes*. Should feel heavy for their size, and have a deep yellow (lemon) or dark green (lime) color. Avoid thick-skinned lemons and soft, wrinkly limes. Or people, for that matter.

- *Oranges*. The heavier the better. You want smooth, thin skins without withered or discolored areas.[2]

- *Peaches*. Should be firm and uniform in color, with a rosy blush. Ripe ones will smell sweet and give under slight pressure.

- *Strawberries*. Should be red, firm, and plump, like a clown's nose. Or a sunburned Danny DeVito.

- *Watermelon*. Two fun ways to check for ripeness. First, scrape the outer rind with your fingernail; you should get a thin green shaving. Second, give it a thump. A ripe watermelon will respond with a hollow thud.

---

[2] You can tell whether the skin is thick or thin by squeezing the fruit slightly. A thinner peel will be much more flexible.

A final note: Because fruits are perishable, they require lots of attention in the store and need to be handled carefully. That means every time you squeeze, poke or shake them, you're possibly damaging the fruit for yourself or the next shopper. So as you check for ripeness, be considerate: Less pestering equals longer life.

THE SPECIFICS: VEGGIES

Mom was right—vegetables are good for you. They're chock-full of nutrients, are naturally low in fat, and fill you up with fiber. Like fruits, fresh vegetables can be identified by their bright, bold colors. They need to be handled carefully to keep bruising to a minimum, and can be safely stored in your fridge for two to five days. Don't buy more than you can use in that amount of time. Some tips:

- *Artichokes*. Seriously, does anyone really eat artichokes?

- *Asparagus*. You want closed, compact tips in a rich green color. Avoid tips that are open, too wide or too long.

- *Broccoli*. Look, just because George Bush senior didn't like them doesn't mean you shouldn't. Buy the ones with tight, dark green (even purplish) buds. Then drape melted cheese over them. Actually, I'd eat shoelaces if you poured enough melted cheese on them.

- *Carrots*. The best ones are smaller: less than six inches in length, an inch in diameter at the widest point, and bright orange. Avoid the really big ones, the soft or flabby ones, and the ones that look "woody." Okay, stop laughing—I know what you're thinking.

- *Corn*. Look for a blunt ear, dark and dry silk, and kernels that spurt juice when you slice them with a fingernail (not that I told you to go around doing that).

- *Lettuce.* Each variety can be different, but generally you want a crisp, non-wilted texture and a good, bright color. Most may have some sort of discoloration on the outer leaves, which is normal, but you should watch out for major decay. Iceberg is the most popular lettuce, but Romaine offers more nutrients and, in my opinion, better taste.

- *Onions.* The best onions are firm, dry, and slightly flat. They should have dry necks and be reasonably free from blemishes (incidentally, this is also the standard to which my sister holds potential suitors). By the way, onions release eye-irritating sulfur compounds when you cut them—that's why they cause tears. The only way to avoid this is to cut them in running water. Or to just stay away from onions.

- *Potatoes.* Potatoes store fairly well, so they can be purchased in bulk. Avoid rot, a greenish tint, sprouts, or sunken eyes.

- *Tomatoes.* The heavier, the better. Ripe tomatoes will be a deep, solid red and yield to pressure. If necessary, they can ripen during storage. Try grape or cherry tomatoes as a snack—they're bite-sized and sweeter than the big ones.

THE SPECIFICS: BEEF AND POULTRY

Now, on to the main course. According to the U.S. Department of Agriculture (USDA), there are three primary grades of beef. USDA Prime is the top-tier stuff because it has the most marbling (the small white specks of fat which make the beef juicier and more flavorful without adding a lot of cholesterol). Most USDA Prime beef is sold to restaurants—rarely will you find it at a grocery store or even a butcher shop. Only two percent of all beef is worthy of this distinction. This is what cows aspire to.

Supermarket beef will usually be graded at the next two levels: USDA Choice and USDA Select. Choice has pretty good marbling (though considerably less than prime) and makes a great steak. USDA Select has the least marbling of the three. It also has fewer calories, but will not be as tender, juicy or flavorful as the others.

Because it's cheaper to buy on the wholesale level, Select is usually what you'll find at the big supercenters or discount stores.

Here's what to look for, besides the label:

- Beef should be a bright red with white flecks of marbling. It should have no gray spots. If the beef has been vacuum-packed, it probably won't turn red until a few minutes after the package is opened— that color is the result of interaction with oxygen.

- Firm is good, mushy is not. Discoloration is not. Lots of extra fat is not. Offensive odors are, obviously, not.

- Check the tray for excess liquid—you don't want it. Because 99 percent of the blood is drained from the carcass at the slaughterhouse, any liquid you see is probably excess moisture that has leaked out.[3] The presence of moisture may indicate the beef has recently been stored at too high of a temperature, allowing bacteria to grow and the taste to decline.

- Check the packaging, too. You don't want torn or punctured plastic wrap. And make sure you're buying before the "sell by" date on the label.

- Beef will keep in your freezer for six to twelve months; ground beef for three months. Wrap it in foil or an airtight plastic bag—not on the plastic tray it comes in—and when you're ready to eat it, thaw it in the fridge to prevent the growth of harmful bacteria.

As for chicken, the easiest way to buy it is in individual cuts—i.e. boneless chicken breasts or individual drumsticks. This can be more expensive than buying an entire chicken, but who wants to do all the separating themselves? Not me. Not you either.

---

[3] It's probably best not to bring up these kinds of factoids during basic dinner table conversation, nor to use the words like "carcass" or "slaughterhouse" in any discussion about meat. People are just sensitive. Just FYI.

A chicken breast should have smooth and tender skin, with well-distributed fat and no blemishes. As usual, avoid torn or damaged packaging. When storing, make sure you keep the chicken refrigerated. To freeze it, remove it from the original packaging and place it in airtight, moisture-proof plastic. Thaw in the fridge or microwave—not at room temperature, as this will kill you. Well, maybe it won't actually kill you, but it will allow harmful bacteria to grow, and you don't want that.

Which brings us right back to our violent beginning. Except in bizarre occurrences of supermarket rage, or if you live under an oppressive totalitarian regime, grocery shopping is rarely a life-and-death-matter. It is, however, an activity that requires a combination of purchasing skill and experience behind the shopping cart. Getting the best value and the freshest produce involves a little time and effort, but it's necessary for those consumers whose culinary tastes have progressed beyond peanut butter and jelly.

And, believe me, that's who you want to be.

HOW TO TAKE CARE OF YOUR HOME

18

Best realization upon moving into my own place: "Hey. I'm still in my underwear and nobody cares!" Worst realization upon moving into my own place: "The toilet's doing what? Where's Dad?"

There are some things that my dad is really good at. Yard work, for instance. Car maintenance. Camping. And taking care of things around the house. Not that he always can fix the leaky dishwasher or rattling furnace, but he can usually tell you what's wrong. Me, I'm lucky if I can find the furnace. After my wife and I purchased our first home a few years ago, I had a sobering thought— the sudden recognition that, in relation to my wife and kids, I was Dad.

Great, um, okay. Now which screwdriver is a Phillips?

Thankfully, I've learned a few things since then, mostly from my dad, my father-in-law, and a good family friend who might as well collect handyman's wages from us. The best piece of advice they've given me? Take care of your home because it sure can't take care of itself. Houses age. They deteriorate. At the same time, they are your largest and most valuable asset and a growing financial investment. The last thing you want is for your home to fall into disrepair.

Everyone remembers the shabby house down the block, the one with the weed-infested yard and the peeling paint and the rusty Nova blocked up in the back. As a homeowner, you don't want this to happen to your place, because even first-graders know those kinds of houses are haunted. Rats. Ghosts. Deranged madmen. Without some basic preventive maintenance, you could find your home in that category. Not good for the resale value.

So accept some advice here from the knowledgeable dads I've

been blessed to learn from: Home maintenance is essential, particularly the preventive kind. It protects your financial investment and property value. It provides a safe, healthy environment for you and your family. And it minimizes repair work and expense—it's a whole lot easier to avoid the development of unsafe conditions and structural damage than to foot the bill once things fall apart.

Your monthly budget should include some money set aside for normal home upkeep. Experts typically suggest putting back 1 to 3 percent of your home's value each year for regular maintenance and the irregular repairs that are needed as your home ages. Every six months you should visually inspect your house and yard to identify trouble spots. Then, make the trouble spots go away. You can always hire professionals to do some tasks, but many precautionary ones are simple enough to do on your own. And much, much cheaper.

Following are some home maintenance tasks to perform on a regular basis. Take note: This is the kind of stuff Dad used to do. If you're under a roof of your own now, male or female, this is now your job.

MONTHLY MAINTENANCE

- Check the pressure gauge on your fire extinguisher, which should be kept near your kitchen stove and any wood-burning fireplace.

- Test smoke detectors and replace batteries if necessary.

- Check your heating and/or cooling air filters. Clean or replace them if necessary. Some filters need to be changed monthly; others are good for three months or more, depending on the type and quality. Check your owner's manual for recommendations.

- Clear gutters and downspouts of debris (leaves, dirt, action figures). Check for loose connections, rust, signs of leakage. Make sure they are properly secured and that there is no blockage in the discharge area.

- Examine shower and/or bathtub enclosures. Replace deteriorated grout and caulk if necessary. Caulk that has become cracked or brittle is useless as a water seal. Remove it and bead on a long-lasting material like silicone or latex. Look for signs of leakage beneath plumbing fixtures. Remove hair from drains (everyone together now: bleeeccchhh) and make sure it drains properly. If not, try a liquid cleaner, an auger (also known as a snake) or a plunger.

- Check all plumbing connections beneath sinks and toilets. Look for leaks at shut-off valves for sinks, toilets, washer and dryer, and the main water shut-off valve. If necessary, replace leaking faucets or showerheads.

- Make sure your toilet flushes correctly, doesn't run continuously (which can occur due to a defective seal) and is properly secured to the floor. Believe me, no one likes a loose potty. Hmm ... maybe I should rephrase that.

- Check ground-fault circuit interrupter devices (known as "GFCI" by the cool kids) in your bathrooms, kitchen, and garage by pressing the test button.

SEASONAL MAINTENANCE (SPRING AND FALL)

- Get up on the roof and look for damage (especially if you live, like I do, in an area where severe late spring and summer thunderstorms can drop golf ball-sized hail). Check for wounded shingles, tiles or other roof coverings, including chimney and flashing. Hint: "Roof flashing" may sound a little perv and possibly criminal, but don't worry—it's just the name for the sheet metal used to reinforce and weatherproof your roof's joints and angles.

- Climb into the attic, if possible, and make sure your roof vents are unobstructed by insulation or anything else. If light from the outside shines through, you're probably okay. Check for vermin activity (according to popular cartoons, mice often collect spools of thread, thimbles and empty sardine tins for furniture, so be on the lookout for artful, domestic arrangements of such). Level out the insulation to cover bare spots, if necessary, and make sure no loose wiring is exposed.

- Give your home exterior a once-over. Trim back tree branches and shrubs so they don't scrape against the house. Take note of any cracked mortar or loose joints in bricks. Check siding for loose or missing pieces, or for cracking and separating on stucco walls. Watch for loose or decaying trim. Make sure all caulking that joins two different materials (such as where window trim meets siding) is in good condition. Do you see peeling, cracked or mildewed paint? Birds' nests? Rival gang graffiti?

- Examine basement or crawl space walls for evidence of moisture seepage, and make sure all landscaping encourages water to flow away from your foundation.

- Inspect all sidewalks, porches, decks, driveways, walkways—you get the idea—for deterioration, cracking, movement, or anything else that can pose a safety hazard. For instance, rattlesnakes.

- Make sure your windows close, lock, and seal properly. Also inspect them for loose putty, holes in screens, and evidence of moisture between pane and storm windows. Look for cracked or broken glass.

- Check the inside and outside of all foundation walls for termite activity. It's a good idea to get an extermination service to do this for you. They know what to look for.

- Test your overhead garage door opener to make

sure the auto-reverse mechanism works. To do so, let it close on a two-by-four, a brick, or a bucket. The door should stop and reverse quickly upon touching the object. If it stops but doesn't reverse, decrease the down-force a quarter-turn or so. Repeat the test until the door reverses. It's also a good idea to clean and lubricate hinges, rollers, and tracks.

ANNUAL MAINTENANCE

- Have your chimney(s) cleaned and inspected each winter before you begin using it regularly. Build-up of soot and creosote can keep it from drafting properly and can potentially cause a chimney fire.

- Look for water damage, exposed wires, or any signs of wear in your electrical service panels. If you have a fuse that blows often or a circuit breaker that trips frequently, call an electrician to figure out the problem and repair it (I'm not usually too eager to work on electrical stuff without professional help). Make sure each circuit is clearly marked so you know what outlets or appliances are connected to it.

- Check the temperature-pressure relief valve on the water heater, which guards against hazardous pressure buildup. Lift up or depress the handle (water should drain from the overflow pipe). Check for signs of leaking or rusting. Some manufacturers recommend that a small amount of water be drained periodically from the tank to reduce sediment buildup. Let it flow into a bucket until the water looks clear.

- Clean and inspect all systems and service appliances as suggested by the manufacturer's recommendations. Some warranties—especially on heating and cooling systems—may be voided if you fail to have an authorized serviceperson inspect them once a year (or as stated otherwise).

- Monitor any wall and ceiling surface cracks for evidence of significant movement. Some minor movement should be anticipated due to normal settling and shrinkage. Large gaps, however, are not normal.

Once during my teenage years, the tape player in my mom's minivan stopped ejecting. The cassette would go in, it would play just fine, but we couldn't get it to come back out. So Dad steps in to fix it.

Fix it he did. After completing what he believed to be one of his most successful projects, Dad called me into the car. "Jason, come check this out," I remember him saying. I watched him proudly demonstrate his triumph by punching the eject button. The tape launched out of the deck—literally—and flew between the two front seats into the floor, ejecting with the velocity of a fighter pilot out of an F-16.

Unfortunately, we could never quite get the now turbo-ejecting cassette deck to actually play after that. It ejected with flair, though. That's the kind of thing I fear when it comes to home maintenance and repair: fixing one thing only to screw up another in the process. So in closing, please realize that it's okay to hire a home repair contractor or handyman to oversee some of the above tips. It's better to pay a little extra for it if the alternative is, for example, two inches of water on your bathroom floor. Don't be afraid to call in the specialists if you're not comfortable with the task.

Preventive maintenance is the key to keeping your house in good shape. It reduces the risk of unexpected repairs while quietly raising your home's resale value. In fact, if you plan to sell some day, it's a good idea to keep a log or journal of all repairs and improvements during your time in the house. By documenting your upkeep regime, you let future owners know the house has been taken care of, and you make sure nothing falls through the cracks.

Speaking of which, by keeping a regular eye out for them—cracks in the foundation, in the mortar, on the walls—you'll be in good shape. Nothing beats a steady system of personal home inspection and repair. Not even walking around in your underwear.

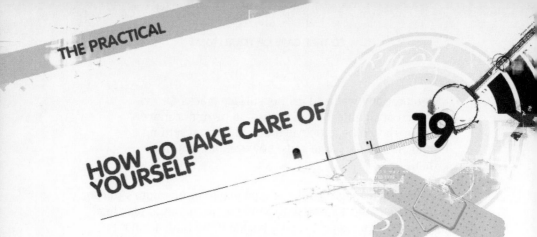

HOW TO TAKE CARE OF YOURSELF

19

In today's streaming video, real-time update, Kraft Easy Mac® society, there's a tiny little aspect of life that tends to get lost in the furious swarm: our health. This world is not one that values rest. When things get really, really busy—Santa Monica Freeway, 5 P.M., "Road Construction Next Seven Miles" busy—sometimes it seems the best advice we can dredge up is from Jimmy the I.T. guy, who suggests downloading that cool new scheduling app for our Palm Pilot®. Call me a Luddite, but I'm not sure Jimmy's who we ought to be turning to for answers. Something seems to be missing, and I have a good idea someone knows what it is.

Let's ask Mom.

Why don't you go outside and get some exercise? Are you getting a good night's sleep? Remember—five servings of fruits and vegetables every day, and make sure you get enough fiber. And don't drink too much coffee.

Maybe we'd all do better to listen to our mothers once in a while. I have a feeling they've been right all along.

Here's an amazing but true story from the AP wire: In July of 2002, a ninety-year-old Austrian beekeeper named Hermann Danner approached his two hives without his usual protective gear. (Now, I know what you're thinking—number one, why isn't this guy playing checkers somewhere in Florida with a bunch of guys named Mortie? And number two, a beekeeper? Yes, a beekeeper. Stay with me.) One would think beekeepers, particularly really old ones, would know not to poke around their hives without, for instance, draping themselves in Kevlar®. But apparently old Mr. Danner didn't get the memo. What he did get was stung.

Repeatedly. When a neighbor finally found him, the old fellow was barely moving. Physicians proceeded to pull nearly one thousand stingers out of his body. Danner told the local media he had tried to defend himself in "a battle that lasted about half an hour but was unsuccessful."

Evidently.

You'll be happy to hear, however, that Hermann Danner made a full recovery and later resumed tending his bees. He can count himself a lucky man—experts generally consider around two hundred stings to be enough to kill a person of that age. If that statement doesn't get your attention, maybe this will: One of the beekeeper's doctors, an allergy specialist, reported that, more than anything else, "Danner's good health had contributed to his speedy recovery."[1]

That's significant. A frail old man, a two-hived bee attack, a thirty-minute battle, and five times the lethal amount of stings. Not only did the guy survive, but he recovered fully and returned to work, all because of his "good health."

Danner must have listened to his mother and kept himself in good health. We'd do well to learn a lesson from this inadequately dressed, fortuitous, and elderly beekeeper. From school assignments or on-the-job projects to family responsibilities and, well, everyday life, we all seem to face a lot of bees. It's easy to lose perspective and approach the hive without protective gear. The result? Our physical, mental, and emotional well-being suffers, and pretty soon we find ourselves being swarmed and stung.[2]

In order to maintain a sense of balance—not to mention control—our best bet is to heed Mom's advice and, for just this once, focus on our own needs. Watch out for number one. Look within. Spend some quality time with your inner child. Insert your own self-help mantra here.

---

[1] Associated Press, "Beekeeper Gets Stung 1,000 Times." ABCNews.com. Posted July 9, 2002.

[2] Just for the record, I'm not talking about real bees or real stinging. These are metaphorical bees; for instance, the "bees of fatigue," or the "bees of the sixty-hour work week," or the "bees of neglected laundry."

It's something you should know by now: Stop neglecting yourself. Here's how.

SLEEP LIKE YOU MEAN IT

Nothing beats a good night's sleep, not even a *Facts of Life* marathon on Nick at Nite. The best way to run yourself to the ground is to let sleep slip down your priority list. Chronic sleep deprivation—even among young, fit twentysomethings—is associated with a number of health problems, including anxiety and depression. It can stress your cardiovascular system, weaken your immune system and throw off your hormone levels. It'll also trash your concentration levels and work performance. Poor sleeping habits have even been linked to heart disease.

So, long story short, it's okay to sleep in a little on Saturdays. In fact, it's probably a good idea. Sundays, too. And the other days of the week, while you're at it. Some helpful hints to ensure you're getting enough sleep:

1) *Wind down before you lie down.* High-quality sleep usually follows a period of relaxation, so take the time to downshift before going to bed. If you exercise at night, do it early enough for your body to cool down and return to restful (in)activity before hitting the sack. Take a hot shower or warm bath. Watch Letterman. Read a book.

2) *Cut the caffeine/nix the nicotine.* Smokes and non-decaf coffee, both stimulants, are to sleep what live monkeys are to a traditional church service: huge disruptions. Even if you don't have trouble falling asleep, the quality of your sleep will suffer if you sip or puff before bed—you'll wake up more often, and you'll take longer to reach the deepest, most restful stage of sleep.

3) *Avoid alcohol and heavy meals.* While a full stomach and a nightcap might make you drowsy, each can keep you from proper rest. Heartburn, indigestion, and even regular digestion can result in frequent awakenings. Same goes for alcohol. While

this doesn't mean you should go to bed on an empty stomach (hunger can keep you up as well), it's wise to schedule the eating and drinking for earlier in the day.

4) *Stick to a schedule.* Our bodies are built to follow patterns, and sleeping is no exception. By going to sleep and waking up at approximately the same times every day, your body eases into a healthy sleep pattern. Staying up till dawn and sleeping extravagantly late on weekends—especially if you do it for two days straight—is like jamming a broomstick into bicycle spokes. Problems ensue. Stuff breaks. And Monday won't be very fun.

5) *Recognize the signs of sleepiness.* Do you have trouble concentrating or making decisions? Are you irritable and moody? Is your memory failing? Maybe you're just not getting enough sleep. Make adjustments: Go to bed earlier, or try to squeeze in a brief catnap during the day.

6) *Check the medical.* Some sleep disorders can't be blamed on a late dinner or weekend rave—they could be the result of a medical problem. Physical conditions like sleep apnea, asthma, and congestive heart failure can inhibit proper sleep. So can common infections or viruses, and even some over-the-counter medications. If you suspect you might have a problem bigger than the after effects of a mug of Folger's before bed, talk to your doctor or a sleep specialist.

EAT GOOD STUFF

Yes, it's very handy to have a Taco Bell within a mile of your home, particularly when you get a refried bean craving at 11 P.M. (now, come on—what did we just say about late-night eating?). And, when it comes down to it, there's really nothing better in life than a slice or four of pepperoni pizza. But, really, the cliché-makers weren't kidding around when they said, "You are what you eat." If you're loading up on fat and grease, don't be surprised when you start to feel fat and greasy. Our generation seriously needs to cut back on the burgers and tacos. Literally, our fast food addiction is killing us (if you don't believe me, I suggest you read Eric Schlosser's unsettling *Fast Food Nation: The Dark Side of the All-American Meal*—you'll never look at a French fry the same way again).[3]

You're a grown up; you probably know how to eat right (though actually doing so is another story). At any rate, let's not spend too much time on this. Just a few reminders:

1) *Eat a variety of nutritious foods.* Carrots are good for you, but not if they're the entirety of your diet. Scientists say we need more than forty different nutrients to maintain good health, but no one food contains all of them. Not even chocolate. Remember the handy food pyramid we learned about in seventh grade health? It still applies. Try to get daily servings of fruits and veggies, bread and whole-grain products, milk and dairy, and some kind of protein (meat, poultry, fish, or—for the vegans among us—protein-rich foods like beans or tofu).

2) *Pay special attention to fruits, vegetables, and whole grains.* Chances are rabbits don't even eat enough of this stuff, so how well can we measure up? Switch out your plain white sandwich bread for whole-grain wheat. Make a smoothie (check out page 181 for more on this). Mix in a salad once in awhile. I've found the absolute best way to make sure you eat enough healthy foods is to keep them handy. When you get the munchies, you're not going to reach for an apple if all you have are Oreos. Stock up on the brain food.

---

[3] Schlosser's book (New York: Harper Collins, 2001) is a fascinating look into the fast food industry, giving particular emphasis to its effects on our bodies and our economy. His argument is that the industry has jammed its grease-stained fingers into every aspect of our lives, from cementing the growth of the modern shopping mall (via the food court) to feeding our country's obesity epidemic. The chapter on food flavoring is as disturbing as it is interesting. Be careful, though: This book has prompted enough dinner-table "did-you-knows" on my part that my wife won't let me bring it up anymore when we go out to eat. It keeps us from enjoying our bacon double-cheeseburgers.

3) *Go easy on the portions.* Heard an interesting fact once. The average plate size in restaurants has increased from eight to twelve inches over the last two decades. What that means is the typical restaurant serving is twice as much as you need. Ladies and gentlemen, meet your new best friend: the doggie bag. Use it. Don't clean your plate at one sitting, and don't eat until you're uncomfortable ("I'm stuffed. I couldn't eat another bite if I—hey, cheesecake!"). Instead, eat half and save the rest for tomorrow. This gives you two meals for the price of one and something to look forward to for lunch the next day.

4) *Don't deprive yourself.* What makes extreme diet changes difficult for most of us is that we eat for pleasure. Food isn't just fuel—it tastes good. Eating healthy doesn't have to mean giving up everything that contains sugar, fat, or cholesterol. It just means limiting your intake. Hot fudge sundaes are fine, but you don't need one after every meal. Bacon? Enjoy, but stop after a couple of slices. Eat what you love, but keep the portions small and the diet balanced.

MANAGE YOUR TIME WISELY

Other than wearing white shoes after Labor Day, the biggest goof we can make is to overburden ourselves with too many commitments. Our schedules are as jam-packed as the Smucker's farm in strawberry season, and the consequence is a cartload of stress. We have too much to do, and too little time to do it. Something's gotta give, and if you're not careful, it'll be you.

Since we all have the same number of hours a day—and since doing away with sleep isn't an option—then the solution to our time crunch must be to learn how to manage what few minutes we have. By learning to work, live, and play more efficiently, we can discover a whole lot more time than we thought possible.

Some tips:

1) *The best minutes of your day are the ones spent planning and organizing.* As a wise man once said—okay, as a poster behind my twelfth grade economics teacher's desk once said—"If you fail to plan, you plan to fail." Any amount of time spent prioritizing and organizing is well spent. Whether it's a simple to-do list or a bells-and-whistles computer program, find what works best for you and stick to it.

2) *Don't procrastinate.* Instead of putting big or difficult tasks off, break them down into smaller, bite-sized pieces. That may mean smaller tasks or shorter periods of time, but at least it means you're doing something.

3) *Combine tasks.* Doing two things at once means double productivity, as long as those two things are compatible. (Note: Driving to work while reading the morning paper are not compatible.) Make to-do lists while you're waiting on hold. Get dressed while you're watching the morning news. Swing by the gas station on your way to the grocery store.

4) *Neglect the trivial.* What's more important: Visiting a friend in the hospital or dusting your PEZ collection? Getting your car's oil changed or watching the last ten minutes of The *A-Team*? (Trust me: The plan comes together.) Stupid examples, but a worthwhile point—by eliminating or postponing the tasks that aren't as necessary or don't have long-term consequences, you clear up time for the things that do.

5) *Be flexible.* Management experts often suggest planning for only 50 percent of your time, because the rest will doubtless be lost to temporary distractions or unplanned urgencies. Expect to be interrupted, but be prepared to get back on track once the disruption's over.

6) *Learn to say no.* This is, in all honesty, my Waterloo. It's hard to turn down friends and family—but it's also hard to get back on track after your schedule is derailed by something unexpected and, in many cases, not really necessary. "No" is such a small word, but it carries a big stick. Using it regularly frees up time for the things that are most important. Don't be selfish, but don't overburden yourself, either.

7) *Enjoy your successes.* The joy of keeping a to-do list is found in the much-anticipated "item cross out." Enjoy it. When you finish a major task, paper, or project, take a moment to relax and strike it from your list. Celebrate the accomplishment. Give yourself a reward. Feel the pressure dissipate like helium from a two-day-old balloon. Such indulgence, even if temporary, nudges you a step closer to a balanced life. And isn't that the goal of time management?

To review, the best ways to take care of yourself are to sleep well, eat well, and manage your time well. Any questions?

No? Then let's return to Hermann Danner and the bees. Those bees can be dangerous if you let them get out of control. But approach them properly (and with the right protective gear) and they'll produce honey. The pressures of life, though intense, can help you become a stronger, more confident person. But when we start to become overwhelmed, our only defense against those pressures is our commitment to the little things that keep us sane. Carving out opportunities to rest, to stay healthy, to manage our lives—these need to be priorities. Without them, we'll find ourselves on the ground, paralyzed, helpless, and feeling old. We'll have fought a good fight, but gotten stung nevertheless.

Yes, the bees are a metaphor, but—never mind. Go eat an apple.

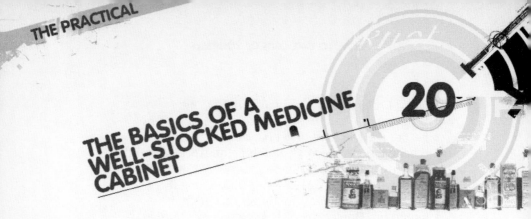

THE BASICS OF A WELL-STOCKED MEDICINE CABINET

20

I love the Brits, and it's not just because of the way they say "schedule." Here's why: Every year, a hard-working governmental entity called the Department of Trade and Industry (DTI) publishes a report detailing the accidents British citizens fall prey to in their own homes. The stated purpose for the Home Accident Surveillance System (HASS) Report is to "help reduce the high toll of serious home accidents in the UK."[1]

By "serious home accidents," of course, the report is referring to injuries sustained via violent collision with one's dog. Not to mention the occasional tea-related scalding, or falls blamed on the deadly combination of tossed-aside underpants and slick, polished floors. You think I'm kidding, but I'm not—the DTI tracks this stuff, and personally, I'm thinking Mr. Rogers might have been advised to swap his comfy cardigan for Kevlar upon entering his home sweet home. You'd be surprised how dangerous life becomes once you leave the stress-filled workplace, exit the traffic-jammed highway, and step in the front door. Consider these statistics from the 1998 report:

- The number of Britons hospitalized (or, I should say, hospitalised) was 130,675 after tripping over their carpet.
- Around 27,000 emergency-room visits each year are slipper-related. Not *slip*-related, mind you, but *slipper*, like the little pink bunny kind.
- Thirty thousand people hurt themselves by falling off a ladder, half of whom were wounded seriously enough to require medical treatment.
- Do-it-yourself tasks were quite perilous, accounting for seventy deaths and one hundred thousand hos-

---

[1] Statistics from DTI Home Safety Network: *www.dti.gov.uk/homesafetynetwork/ gh_intro.htm.*

pital visits on a yearly basis. Misuse of tools—particularly saws and knives—was the biggest culprit.
• Candle calamities sparked more than 1,700 fires, which subsequently resulted in 772 injuries and eleven deaths.[2]

Are the British that clumsy? Yes, possibly. But not any more so than Americans. They're just more efficient in tracking this sort of thing, recognizing the inherent dangers in, for instance, flowerpots and pants. You know they say that 90 percent of all accidents happen within five miles of your home? What they forget to mention is that most of these actually occur inside the home, and evidently saucepans are usually to blame.

All of which brings me to this conclusion: Everyone who lives somewhere—homeowners, apartment dwellers, moochers subsisting on their parents' dime—needs to be fully prepared to deal with injuries and illnesses that take place in the home. That means you need a decent medicine cabinet, properly stocked and ready for any accident—no matter how bizarre. How to achieve this is something you should know by now.

Let's get to the details.

THE STUFF YOU NEED

• *Minor injury supplies*. Say you trip over your carpet and, um, cut your knee on a saw blade (silly Brit!). You don't want to then limp all around the house, trailing blood like a stuck pig while searching for a couple of Band-Aids®. Your medicine cabinet should have all the basics of minor wound management, including adhesive bandages, gauze, and sterile tape, hydrogen peroxide (the fun stuff that bubbles as it cleans the nasty germs out of your wound), and an ice pack. FYI: A bag of frozen peas also makes an effective ice pack, just in case. But it looks weird.

---

[2] "Warning: Your Pants Can Kill," *The Guardian Unlimited* (Posted May 30, 2000, at *www.guardian.co.uk/health/story/0,3605,319998,00.html*).

- *Pain reliever/fever reducer*. Most professionals recommend keeping two types of pain relief products on hand. One should be an ibuprofen-based or aspirin product that acts as an anti-inflammatory—these are ideal for toothaches, muscle pulls, menstrual cramps, arthritis, etc. The other should be a non-aspirin pain reliever like Tylenol®, which is most effective for general aches and pains, fever reduction, and headaches.
- *Antibiotic ointment*. A triple antibiotic cream, such as the Neosporin® brand name, is the best infection protection available for minor cuts and scrapes. It promotes faster, germ-free healing—simply apply a thin coat beneath a bandage.
- *Pepto-Bismol®* or its equivalent. No one likes to talk about it, but at some point we all get a rumble in the belly. A product to treat diarrhea, nausea, indigestion, and heartburn is essential.
- *Syrup of Ipecac*. Pray you never have to use this, but keep it on hand just in case. Ipecac is used to induce vomiting in case of accidental poisoning or ingestion of an unknown product. Important: Use it only after calling poison control and being instructed to do so. Some chemicals like bleach or other corrosives do greater harm on the way back up than they do going down.
- *Decongestants and antihistamines*. These are the products that relieve cold and allergy symptoms. Some professionals only recommend buying cold and cough medicines when they're needed, since there are so many varieties. That's your call. If you suffer often from allergies, then it makes sense to keep an over-the-counter antihistamine on hand. Same for those who deal with perpetually stuffy noses.
- *Cough medicines*. There are two kinds: suppressants and expectorants. Cough suppressants help quiet the kind of dry, irritating cough that keeps you up at night and annoys your friends. Expectorants help loosen chest congestion (also known, delicately, as "inducing phlegm"). Though a little unpleasant, this kind of coughing helps clear

all that extra infection-prone phlegm from your lungs, so it's a good thing to do. Many cough medicines combine a suppressant and expectorant into a single dose. Please note: These types of over-the-counter meds are intended for minor coughs only. If you have one that persists for more than a few days, see a doctor.

- *Hydrocortisone cream.* Probably the strongest anti-itching cream available, so keep this around to treat skin rashes or itchiness due to minor irritations and inflammations, eczema, insect bites, poison ivy, etc.
- *Tweezers.* For splinters, in case you were wondering. A magnifying glass also helps. And while we're on the subject, here's a secret: One of the least painful and most effective means of splinter removal is to apply clear tape to the area and then carefully peeling it off. Don't tell anyone I told you.
- *Thermometer.* These days, they're more expensive than the ones Mom used to pop in your mouth when you were feeling bad, but you really can't beat a good digital thermometer. The digital ones are much faster (taking seconds instead of minutes), more accurate, and easier to use and read than the old oral stand-bys. A good one is worth the investment, especially if you have kids.
- *Sunscreen.* Call me crazy, but pasty and white is better than wrinkled and cancerous any day. Minimum SPF should be 15.
- *First-aid manual.* Unless, of course, you've memorized one.

THE STUFF YOU DON'T NEED

- *Expired medications.* Some products lose their potency as they age, but a few liquid meds may begin to evaporate and become more powerful. It doesn't happen automatically at the expiration date, but it's safest not to take a chance.
- *Old prescriptions.* Anything you've had more than two years is suspect. It's tempting to save half-used prescriptions for ailments you no longer have, just in case you get sick again. But self-medication is

generally a bad idea and can sometimes do more harm than good. Toss the old stuff.

- *Any medicine that has begun to degrade*, discolor, separate, or form a gooey residue.
- *Any medicine that has been damaged* by water leaks.
- *Hydrogen peroxide* that refuses to bubble.
- *Aspirin* that crumbles or smells vinegary.
- *Any unlabeled medicine* or medicine prescribed for someone else.
- *Condoms past their expiration date.* Most are good for four to five years past the date of manufacture, and don't just fall into pieces once they expire. But the name of the game is safety, right? Incidentally, condoms with spermicides are good for only eighteen months to two years, which is the expiration of the spermicide.

STUFF YOU MIGHT NOT HAVE CONSIDERED BUT SHOULD

- *Green tea.* The ancient Chinese and Japanese used to regard green tea as a medicine, and we're just now beginning to understand why. Though not used as a specific remedy for any diseases, scientists keep discovering health benefits associated with the product. Green tea contains a powerful antioxidant compound called polyphenol. Scientists believe that polyphenols help prevent cancer from forming and may shrink cancer cells that are already present. Green tea may also protect against heart disease, boost the immune system, prevent the formulation of blood clots and strokes and even protect against digestive and respiratory infections. There's also evidence it may help avoid cavities, reduce cholesterol, and give you X-ray vision. Okay, that last one is a stretch, but green tea is practically a super-powered beverage. While the scientific jury is still out—results are so far inconclusive—I'd make a hot mug of green tea part of my daily routine. (Incidentally, some forms of non-herbal black teas also contain polyphenols, but in smaller amounts.)
- *Vitamin C supplements.* Recent research has discov-

ered a link between vitamin C deficiency and a number of health problems, including cataracts, stomach and esophageal cancer, and rheumatoid arthritis. A lack of vitamin C can also lead to minor annoyances like nosebleeds, easy bruising, and bleeding gums. Regarding the common cold, vitamin C probably won't prevent it, but scientists are starting to find that a large dose of it (five hundred to one thousand milligrams a day) may lessen its symptoms and decrease its duration. You can get your minimum daily allowance of Vitamin C by drinking orange juice and eating fresh strawberries, oranges, and grapefruit, or you can take one of the countless vitamin C supplements on the market.

- *Soap and sanitizing gels*. Speaking of colds, we all walk around with bacteria on our hands, and when we touch doorknobs and water faucets and soft drink machines we're depositing our germs and collecting others'. Yuck. Regular hand washings are the best way to fight this. They keep germs and the diseases they cause from spreading. The Centers for Disease Control and Prevention recommend rigorously scrubbing your hands in warm water for at least fifteen seconds to remove germs. If soap's not readily available, an antibacterial "hand sanitizer" gel will do the trick, all while making you smell like vanilla mango or something equally girly.[3]

A few final thoughts on medicine cabinets. Too keep it from becoming a burial ground for old prescription bottles, degraded creams, and yellowed bandages, give your medicine stash a good reorganization once every year or so. Out with the old and in with

---

[3] And another warning: Our love of antibacterial products may be in danger of being taken too far. For one thing, many diseases are viral in nature, and antibacterial soap doesn't have any effect on them. Secondly, some bacteria are good for us, but we're killing them off with all our mango-smelling soap. Thirdly, scientists have warned that all this use of bacteria-killing agents may lead to the development of bacterial "superbugs" over the long-term–really, really bad germs that are resistant to our soaps and gels. Furthermore, in October 2002, researchers released the results of a study finding that soaps with antibacterial compounds don't work any better than regular soap products in killing germs. Source: Jim Ritter, "Anti-Germ Soap No Better Than Plain Kind," *Chicago Sun-Times* (Posted October 24, 2002, at *www.suntimes.com/output/health/cst-nws-soap24.html*).

the new, so to speak. And contrary to popular belief, the bathroom really isn't the best place to keep your medicine cabinet. Most medical products store best in cool, dry environments, not warm and humid ones like the bathroom or some kitchens. Consider collecting everything in a big plastic container and storing it on the top shelf of an interior closet—make sure it's easy for you to access but out of the reach of children.

Ideally, your home medicine cabinet should be ready for any minor emergency. It should be well organized, easy-to-access, and regularly updated. Because you can never be too prepared when surrounded at all times by such dangerous household products as socks and pants.

21

THE IMPORTANCE OF FOOD SAFETY

My wife thinks I'm a freak. There are several reasons this is so—too many really to get into it, as most husbands will tell you—but a majority of them have something to do with eating and drinking. For one thing, I'm a Dr. Pepper snob. To the irritation of most members of my family, I insist on drinking the soft drink chilled, over ice, and in a glass (plastic simply will not do; nor will a room-temperature D.P., even when poured over ice). I'll have it no other way. Civilization requires its standards.

I also take any store-bought salsa and put it in a blender. After having given it a good whirl—because salsa ought to be finely chopped—I top it off with a little salt. Always. Furthermore, I prefer my bananas slightly green and find store-bought hot chocolate mix (dry) to be one of the world's most underrated toppings for vanilla ice cream.

But those aren't the only reasons my wife raises her eyebrow at me in the kitchen. I have another borderline-OCD issue: I'm adamant about food safety. I wash my hands before and after handling food. I refrigerate leftovers quickly. I keep raw stuff off the counter and know how hot a grilled steak needs to be before it's done. I'm a food safety commando.

I'm not exactly sure how this began. It may have something to do with the fact that I know of several occasions when I got sick, without a doubt, from eating bad food. Tromping in and out of a fly-ridden outhouse is a good way to ruin a Colorado fishing trip. Maybe it's because I've spent a significant portion of my professional life writing and designing marketing materials for a regional supermarket chain, one that's committed to educating its employees and customers about food borne illness and prevention.

Whatever the reason, food safety is in my blood. And as a result of my diligence, that freakish blood stays pretty clear of bacterial microbes. So there.

THE FACTS

The Centers for Disease Control (CDC) in Atlanta, Georgia, estimates that 76 million cases of food borne illness occur every year in the United States. Most of these cases are mild—the afflicted might suffer from flu-like symptoms for a day or two (stomach cramps, diarrhea, and fever are all associated with food poisoning). But some illnesses go a little further than that. An estimated 325,000 cases require hospital visits each year. And on a yearly basis, up to five thousand people die from some form of food poisoning.[1]

To put that into perspective, let's compare it with something else most Americans have experienced to one degree or another—automobile accidents. According to the Federal Highway Administration, there were an estimated 6.3 million car wrecks in the U.S. in 2001. That's less than one-tenth the amount of food borne illnesses. Granted, more people are injured from vehicular accidents every year (more than three million), but those kinds of wrecks aren't nearly as common as the culinary ones.[2]

Food borne illnesses occur when bacteria are given a chance to thrive in a warm, moist environment. It follows that certain foods, then, provide a great starting point, especially those high in protein and moisture. Milk and dairy products, eggs, meat, poultry, fish, and anything containing any combination of these products are highly susceptible to bacterial growth. These are all healthy foods and good for you to eat, but mishandling them can lead to trouble.

To top it off, when food poisoning does occur, it's hard to pin-

---

[1] "Foodborne Infections," Centers for Disease Control and Prevention Online, Division of Bacterial and Mycotic Diseases: Disease Information, updated October 1, 2002 (*www.cdc.gov/ncidod/dbmd/diseaseinfo/foodborneinfections_g.htm*).
[2] "2001 Annual Assessment of Motor Vehicle Crashes," National Center for Statistics and Analysis, updated October 2002 (*http://www-nrd.nhtsa.dot.gov/pdf/nrd-30/NCSA/Rpts/2002/Assess01.pdf*).

point exactly what has caused it and when. Sometimes symptoms show up immediately. Other times, they can take several days to make their way through your system, making it difficult to identify the culprit. So how do you prevent food borne illness? Just like you try to prevent injury in a car wreck—by making safety a habitual part of your driving. You pay attention to the road and to other drivers. You strap on a safety belt. You keep your tires properly inflated. Food safety is the same way. By making a habit of it, you can keep a bad batch of chicken salad from causing a gastrointestinal wreck. Here are some food safety tips and procedures you should know:

KEEP HOT FOOD HOT

In eighth grade home economics, many of us were told it's a good idea to let leftover foods cool down before stashing them in the fridge, in order to keep the refrigerator from having to expend so much energy in cooling them down. Little did we know that the home ec teacher was trying to kill us. She was aged and married, so I should have known: old wives' tale. Not a good idea. Leaving hot food on the counter until it cools to room temperature is like wearing a Justin Timberlake shirt to OzzFest—it's an invitation for something unfortunate to happen.

Here are two numbers you should remember: forty degrees and 140 degrees. The space between those temperatures is the happy zone for bacterial growth. At these temps, bacteria multiply like bunnies. Therefore, you need to keep your hot foods above the safe temperature of 140 degrees Fahrenheit, which is too warm for bacteria to do much more than sit around complaining about the heat. That means eating your pizza within two hours of delivery. Or refrigerating uneaten hamburger patties within two hours of taking them off the grill (one hour if you're outside on a summer day). The same goes for any other leftovers—find a place for them in the fridge as soon as you clear the table.

KEEP COLD FOOD COLD

Same concept, different direction. This will make you feel good inside: Raw ground beef and poultry products (including eggs) often already contain illness-causing bacteria like E. coli or salmonella, respectively—even while on the shelf at the neighborhood grocery store. Yes, friends, they come that way. Not to worry, though—these latent bacteria are destroyed when you cook foods thoroughly. And when frozen or refrigerated, the microbes are practically paralyzed.

That's why meat and poultry should stay in the fridge until you're ready to cook. That's also why great care should be taken on picnics, camping trips, or when grilling out to make sure your cooler stays cool. Fill it full of ice or frozen gel packs. Keep it out of the direct sun. Keep the lid closed, and avoid leaving lunchmeats, potato salads, pasta salads, meat, chicken, and other perishables out of the cooler for very long. If you fail in this regard, bite the bullet and toss out the offending food. Better to do without another chicken salad sandwich than to spend the next day, well, you know ...

AVOID CROSS-CONTAMINATION

As stated above, before meat and poultry are cooked (and the microorganisms in them killed) they could be harboring illness-causing bacteria. That's why it's important to keep them from cross-contaminating other foods or utensils before they're cooked. This is probably the area of food safety wherein people are the most careless, so pay attention.

The best thing to do when it comes to raw meat or poultry is to separate. Keep them away from other foods—in your grocery cart, in your refrigerator, on your kitchen counter. Don't slice raw chicken on a cutting board, and then plop down a head of lettuce right where the chicken was. Unless you washed the cutting board with soap and warm water between foods, you've just contaminated your broccoli. Shame on you. You should know better by now.

Same goes for serving platters and utensils. Don't take a plate full of raw sirloins out to the grill, fire things up, and then put the cooked steaks back on the same juicy plate. Leftover bacteria on the platter could contaminate the safely cooked food. Another rule: Never taste or reuse the marinade in which you've already soaked raw meat, poultry, or seafood, unless you boil it first. (If you intend to use it later as a sauce, just keep some of it separate from the raw food.) You'll also want to pay close attention to the arrangement of food in your freezer and refrigerator. There's nothing worse than raw chicken juice dripping onto your apple pie. Actually, there are some things worse—like flesh-eating bacteria or movies starring Dana Carvey—but I don't want to go there. That's another chapter, another book.

THAW SAFELY

Here's another example of motherly advice gone wrong. Don't thaw frozen food in the sink, on the counter, out on the sidewalk, or anywhere other than the refrigerator or the microwave. I refer you back to the 40/140 rule—you don't want raw foods sitting around in the danger zone, which is exactly what happens if you thaw a slab of frozen ground beef at room temperature. Don't do it, even if Mom used to thaw the Thanksgiving turkey in the bathtub. It's just plain wrong.

The safest way to thaw is to let the frozen food defrost slowly in the fridge. If you forget to plan far enough ahead to do this, it's okay to use the defrost setting on the microwave, as long as you cook the food immediately afterward.

KEEP STUFF CLEAN

This one's obvious, right? You'd think so. Most people are smart enough not to handle raw chicken and then, for instance, lick the bacteria-laden poultry juice off their hands. But what you might not realize is that our hands also have bacterial microbes on them all the time—even before handling raw foods—and for that reason, it's just as easy for us to transfer bacteria to the chicken, where it can spring to life and start reproducing wildly (the bacteria, mind you, not the chicken; frankly, that would be disturbing). So wash your hands with warm, soapy water both before and after handling raw meat, poultry, and seafood. Wash any utensils, including meat thermometers and grilling tools. Same goes for serving platters, cutting boards and any other surfaces that come into contact with raw foods. Pay particular attention to your sink and kitchen counter, places where other foods are likely to be prepared.

Food safety is all about risk management. By handling food properly, you can significantly decrease your risk of exposure to food borne illness. While there's no reason to become obsessive or

paranoid about it—inspecting every bite of chicken, for example, to make sure it's fully cooked—there's also no reason not to make the above tips part of your daily kitchen or outdoor grilling routine. A delicious meal (accompanied by a properly chilled glass of Dr. Pepper) is one of life's great joys. That joy decreases exponentially when it results in fever, vomiting, and general intestinal difficulties.

So be safe. Follow the rules. And no more snacking on raw chicken.

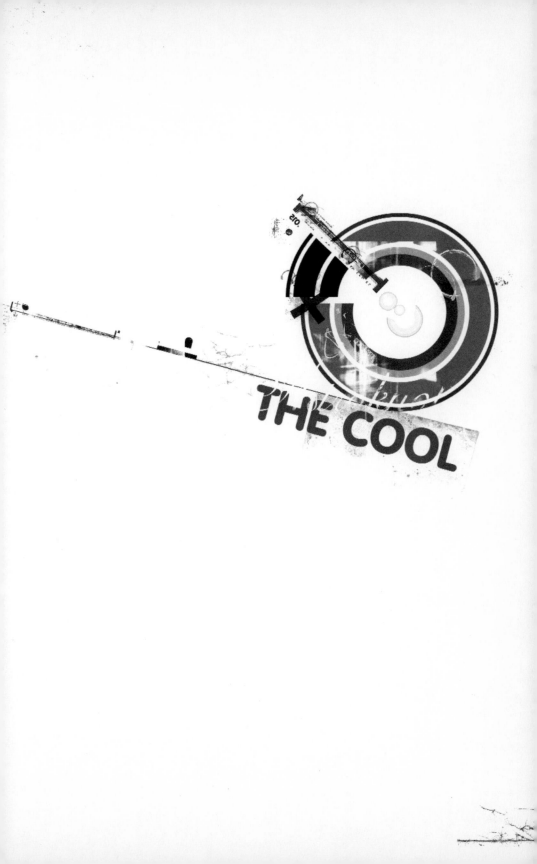

THE COOL

22 HOW TO PLAY A LITTLE POKER

"You were lookin' for that third three, but you forgot that Professor Green folded on Fourth Street and now you're representing that you have it. The DA made his two pair, but he knows they're no good. Judge Kaplan was trying to squeeze out a diamond flush but he came up short and Mr. Eisen is futilely hoping that his queens are going to stand up. So like I said, the Dean's bet is twenty dollars."

The above quotation, lifted from lines spoken by Matt Damon's cardsharp protagonist in the 1998 poker flick, Rounders, makes about as much sense to a gaming virgin as a Palm Pilot does to an Amish blacksmith. Sheesh—I know a little bit about the game (enough to write about it, at least), but still don't have any idea what he's talking about.

Such is the appeal and intimidation of poker, like the two sides of a quarter. Those who are in the know can feel part of an elite group, speaking their own language, chronicling tells, assailing bluffs, calculating risks that laymen don't even know exist. If you've ever met a poker aficionado, you'll know that his version of the game can be all-consuming. For these, poker is a culture. So, lesson number one: Never play poker with someone who says anything like, "That sucker made a crying call on a deuce-to-seven." The lingo should tip you off: You'll lose your money, the deed to your house, or your left kidney. Let those guys school someone else.

But don't let that keep you from enjoying a game that's as gaudily American as Vegas. Poker is unique in that it blends chance and skill, confidence, and competition into a social activity unmatched by most other pastimes. Play at home with your friends, and the resulting combination of low-end wagering, friendly atmosphere, and limitless game variations guarantees a fun evening, with or without the beer (which, lesson number two, is often not the best beverage to consume when gambling). Unless it's cutthroat World Series of Poker-style competition, poker is a social diversion and meant to be enjoyed as such.

So following are some things you should know about poker before being dealt in. Keep in mind that, while these are general rules that apply in most poker games, the game has hundreds of tweaks and variations—and an anything-goes mentality that depends largely on house rules. Regardless, the following are more or less undeniable:

THE BASICS

Poker is played with a full deck of fifty-two cards, ranked from Ace to Ace. The game is typically played with each player being dealt five cards; whoever holds the highest cards at the end wins. From low to high, the hierarchy is: Ace, Two, Three, Four, Five, Six, Seven, Eight, Nine, Ten, Jack, Queen, King, Ace. The ace can be either high or low depending on the hand, but never both in the same hand.

Poker is a democratic game. Suits (Clubs, Diamonds, Hearts, Spades) matter on some occasions, but none is considered higher than another.

WHAT BEATS WHAT

How do you determine who has the highest hand? Simple. Follow the hierarchy. Knowing this sequence is one of the best steps you can take toward understanding the game. After all, if you don't know what's supposed to happen after everyone displays their cards, you might as well go back to Solitaire. Here's the list from top to bottom:

Royal Flush. The five highest cards of the same suit (Ace, King, Queen, Jack, Ten). This is the Holy Grail of poker—it can't be beaten in a non-wild-card game. Odds of being dealt this hand in five cards are one in 650,000. So if you get it twice in a row, you're probably cheating.

Straight Flush. Same as above (a Royal Flush is a Straight Flush), but it doesn't have to be face cards. An Ace can be high or low; wraparound is not allowed (i.e. King, Ace, 2, 3, 4). A straight is no royal flush, but it's still impressive.

Four-of-a-Kind: Four cards with the same number or face ranking. Someone would have to have an unbelievable hand to take on a Four, so bet on it.

Full House: A remarkably long-running television show featuring noted thespians Dave Coulier, John Stamos, and a handful of cute little girls. Or, in poker, three cards of a kind combined with a pair. Still a great hand to get, but there's always a chance someone else will also have a full house. If this occurs, a tie is broken by whomever has the higher-ranking triplet.

Flush: Any five nonconsecutive cards of the same suit. Make sure you're matching suit and not just color (for example, mixing in a diamond among a four-card flush of hearts). Poker players have a word for that: Dumb. You'll be mocked, and they'll take your money.

Straight: A straight of cards, as above, only this time they don't have to be the same suit. Ace can be high or low, and no wrap-around allowed. The straight with the highest card wins the tiebreaker.

Three-of-a-Kind: Three cards of any rank (plus two more non-matching cards). Highest three of a kind wins in the event of a tie.

Two pair: See where we're going with this? High pair wins in a tie.

One pair: Loser.

High card: The person holding the highest card when no one else has absolutely anything.

THE MOST POPULAR VARIATIONS

5-Card Draw: The basic game. Deal five cards facedown to each player. There is an initial betting round, then each player is allowed to trade one, two, or three cards with the deck (three is

the max). Another betting round follows.

5-Card Stud: The basic game, but with a cool-sounding name and a twist. Dealing sequence can vary, but it usually provides each player with two cards facedown on the table and three cards, eventually, face-up (five cards total). The betting round begins with the high hand after the first three cards have been dealt (two down, one up). Then, another card is dealt, followed by another betting round. Repeat for final card.

7-Card Stud: Same as above, only using seven cards in a combination of three down, four up. Winner has the best hand using the five best cards out of his or her seven.

Lowball: Five cards are dealt to each player following the rules of 5-Card Draw—except this time, you're trying for the worst hand. A good game to suggest when you find yourself folding every other hand.

Texas Hold'em: This is the game played by the Poker deities at high-stakes venues; it's world series stuff and pretty complex, so be cautious when it's suggested. Deal two cards face down to each player (these are called "Hole" or "Pocket" cards). A round of betting commences (often a blind bet, made before seeing your cards—again, serious stuff). Then, three cards are dealt face-up in the middle of the table. This is called the "flop." Don't ask why. There is a round of betting, based on your two pocket cards and the three flop cards. Another card is added to the flop (this one's called the "turn"). Another round of betting. Finally, a fifth card (the "river"), and a final round of betting. You make your best hand based on your two pocket cards and any three cards in the community flop. In casinos, this can be a very expensive game, with the pot doubling or tripling on the turn and river bets. It can be very complicated. A good rule is to never play with people who say "flop," "turn," or "river," unless they're into whitewater rafting.

HOW THE BETTING WORKS

After the dealer announces which version of the game is to be played—but before the cards are dealt—all players must "ante-up" by tossing the minimum table bet (the "ante") into the pot. This predetermined amount ensures that everyone playing has some stake in the game. By not anteing, you either indicate that you don't understand the game being played or you aren't participating in this round. Or you're flat out of money, which indicates you should have left about an hour ago.

The player to the left of the dealer typically opens the betting (though he may "check," or pass that privilege to the next player, if he chooses). After the betting is opened—let's say with a dime— it then moves to the next person at the table to continue. This person has three options. She can:

1) *See the bet and call*, which at the start of the game means matching the amount of the previous bet. In the example above, the player would wager a dime since the game and betting has just begun. In the next betting round, she'll need to meet the amount the bet has been raised since her most recent wager. If it raises at any point before returning to her, she'll have to calculate and pay that amount.

2) *Raise the bet*, meaning she not only matches the previous bet, but adds to it. In this example, she would see the bet with a dime and raise it a nickel. This makes it more expensive for others to remain in the game. There is usually a limit to the amount you can raise a bet.

3) *Fold*, like a paper airplane in the grubby hands of a nine year old. If you have a lousy hand, folding lets you out of the game. You forfeit the chance to win the pot, but you don't have to worry about losing any more than your ante. To fold, simply place your cards face down on the table, and say, "I fold." Add a measure of disgust to your voice, and you might get sympathy.

Betting keeps everyone honest by increasing the pot while keeping players with bad hands from the opportunity to win. Generally, those players who participate in the betting process are reasonably confident they have a chance to come out on top. Unless, of course, they're bluffing—which is basically a nice way to say "lying," when your cards have no real chance of winning—in order to make other players mistakenly believe they have a high hand. The bluffing player's only hope is that an initial high bet scares everyone off. Then they take the pot. Unless you're really, really good at poker, this probably won't work. Besides, no one likes a liar.

The only way to stay in a game is not to fold, so if you're ever going to win a pot in poker, you're going to need to understand how and when to bet. If you have a bad hand, you should fold. If you have the makings of a good hand, just needing to replace one or two cards with new ones, then you should consider staying in. If you were just dealt a full house, or a straight flush, or four Kings, you should definitely stay in. Just don't start giggling like a schoolgirl or bouncing in your chair or giving some other signal that you're sitting on a sure thing.[1] If the rest of the players pick up on this, they'll fold and all you'll get with your once-in-a-blue-moon hand is the ante. Woo hoo. Play it cool, raise the betting with restraint, and see what happens.

The wagering aspect of poker—when to bet, how much to bet, and how to increase the pot without practically saying "Lookee! I've got a full house!"—isn't the kind of thing that's easily explained in a book. (Lord knows I've given it a good shot, though. Right? Am I right? Come on, give me some love.) The fact is, you're gonna have to learn by playing. Find some buddies who know the game but are nice enough not to take advantage of your ignorance and play. Keep it low-stakes, or no stakes at all—when I was a kid, my cousins and I used to play poker while betting with Skittles candies. Reds were the ante. We thought we were pretty cool.

Poker can be a fun game, and it's even more fun when you add a little money into the mix. It doesn't have to be much—a nickel, dime, or quarter ante is a great place to start. In fact, I won't play if the stakes are higher than that. High-stakes poker is much more stressful and therefore, much less fun. The best advice when play-

---

[1] This inadvertent mannerism—a subtle physical clue that you have a good hand—is called a "tell," and experienced poker players learn to watch for them while hiding tells of their own. The trick is to be as stone-faced as possible when appraising your cards. Unless, of course, you're jittery all the time, in which case a serene, emotionless poker face would so abnormal as to indicate something's up. Yep, tells can be tricky.

ing poker? Keep it light, loose, and social.

And never, never, never play with anyone called Ace, Slim, or Jimmy the Blade. In fact, it's generally a good idea not to partici-pate in any sort of activity with anyone nicknamed "the Blade."

Just so you'll know ...

HOW TO PERFORM AN AMAZING CARD TRICK

23

In May of 1997, magicians the world over flew into fits of rage upon viewing a network television special called David Blaine: Street Magic. The program followed an unknown sleight-of-hand upstart as he strolled the sidewalks of New York City and Atlantic City doing decent but very basic magic and card tricks. Audiences had a different response. Whether watching from the safety of their living rooms or watching him live from a few feet away, Blaine's audience was enthralled. Viewers were treated to shots of his spectators screaming and gasping and pointing in disbelief, particularly following some apparent self-levitation stunts.

Magicians, however, hated him. They still do.[1] In their eyes, his tricks were pedestrian, stuff any magician worth his or her salt could pull off. And Blaine was the beneficiary, they suspected, from some television trickery. You know how they say the camera adds ten pounds? Apparently it also adds two feet to levitation stunts.

Nevertheless, David Blaine went from unknown twentysomething street performer to Quasi-Celebrity, Network Television Darling, and Friend of Leo within a matter of months. Why? No one knows. It's magic! (Cue woo-woo music.)

Actually, it's quite explainable: David Blaine is an expert at projecting mystery. He's a riddle wrapped in an enigma and smothered in secret sauce. It's all in the demeanor. Blaine is moderately multi-culti handsome, but nothing special. His voice is a low-key

---

[1] Especially now that Blaine has added "published author" to his resume. His book, *Mysterious Stranger*–part autobiography, part magic how-to, part self-help tome–was released in October of 2002 to moderate acclaim.

monotone, and his hangdog eyes are lifeless. Upon entering a room, he's probably the last person you'd expect to be the life of the party.

That is, until he whips out a pack of cards, at which point, he becomes David Blaine, mystifying and hypnotic and cool. Not shopping mall cool, which is as easy to come by as fifty bucks and a new pair of shoes. Not cultural cool, which you can become by dropping the names of the right bands at the right time in the right place. Not any kind of easily attainable cool, but something else entirely: the kind of cool that makes it clear that you know more than anyone else in the room. Or in Blaine's case, knowing more than anyone else on the sidewalk in front of McSorley's, East 7th.

Blaine's rep has been built almost entirely on the mystical/spooky aura he projects while performing mundane "Is this your card?" tricks to the delight of his flabbergasted subjects. That's the power of "magic."

And that's why one of the first steps toward establishing your coolness is learning how to perform a decent card trick. It'll take a little practice, some refined mid-trick patter and more than a little attitude, but you, too, can be as cool as David Blaine. Figuratively speaking, of course. Because you wouldn't want to literally be that cool—this is a guy, you'll remember, who spent several days encased in a big chunk of ice as a publicity stunt—er, amazing feat of endurance.

So here's something you should know by now: how to astonish your friends and startle your enemies with a simple card trick. The trick? It's known in the magic world by several names, including Find the Card, the 21-Card Trick, the Eleventh Card, or Sim Sala Bim. It works due to a mathematical principle rather than a stacked deck or sleight-of-hand, so anyone can master it almost immediately and perform it in an impromptu setting. And when you do it right, it always works. So pay attention—you're about a thousand words away from being respectably cool.

PART THE FIRST: THE SETUP

The goal is to have the spectator pick out a card from a set of

twenty-one. You won't be told specifically which card it is, but you'll eventually find out. From there, you'll be able to reveal your knowledge via a number of mind-boggling scenarios. It's quite the puzzler.

1) Begin with twenty-one cards out of any deck. Doesn't matter which cards they are—any twenty-one will do. For credibility's sake, you might let your audience count out the initial twenty-one cards for you, in order to keep you from any pre-trick monkey business. Not that you'd need it.

2) Deal the cards, face-up, into three vertical columns of seven cards each. Distribute the cards horizontally: Card 1, Card 2, Card 3. Card 4 is laid in the same column as Card 1, overlapping it slightly. Card 5 overlaps Card 2, and so on. Continue until you've dealt out all twenty-one cards into three columns, seven cards deep. The dealing sequence is important to the trick, so don't accidentally deal two cards at once or distribute the cards top-to-bottom instead of across.

3) Ask someone to mentally select a card from one of the columns. Then have him indicate which column his card is resting in—left, middle, or right. You don't need to know suit, number, or anything else. Only the column.

4) Once the column has been indicated, square the three columns up (this is done much more easily when the cards overlap) and stack them together. The spectator's column must be placed between the other two. For instance, if he indicates Column C, then assemble them in your hand with A on bottom, C in the middle, and B on top. Do this quickly and without fanfare and your spectator won't notice you've reordered the columns.

5) Deal them out again, same procedure as step two. Again, have the person indicate which column his chosen card appears in. Then square them up and stack them together—the spectator's column goes between the other two.

6) Deal out the cards once again, same procedure, and have the person indicate his column. He will point

to the middle column, and the card he chose at the beginning of the trick will be the card—card number eleven—in the exact middle of the group of twenty-one. Take note of this card, then gather them up in order.[2]

So here's what you've got, Captain Remarkable: A stack of twenty-one cards, and the card your spectator chose is the eleventh from the top (and, as it were, the eleventh from the bottom). You've arrived at this card via the wonders of a mathematical principle. It's a long, intricate explanation, using a combination of algebraic formulas that a) I'm too lazy to take the time to understand; and b) I'm not interested in going into anyway. I doubt you feel much differently. So just trust me on this—by making three piles three times, and keeping the indicated pile in the middle of the pack, you automatically place the card they chose in the center of your twenty-one-card deck. There will be ten cards ahead of it and ten cards behind.

PART THE SECOND: THE PAYOFF

The hard part is finished; all that remains is the astonishing revelation. What you do next depends on how tricky you want to be. A number of "reveals" are available to you, variations on ways to show the spectator his eleventh card. Like most things in life, the more creative the reveal, the better. Here are three options:

Easiest. Pick a word or phrase that consists of either ten or eleven letters, then deal out one card per letter, stopping with the selected eleventh card. For instance, you can use the ten-letter phrase "Y-O-U-R C-A-R-D I-S," revealing the eleventh card after you've finished spelling. Or, choose an eleven-letter word like Abracadabra and spell it out: "A-B-R-A-C-A-D-A-B-R-A," wherein the card is exposed on the final "A." While any eleven-letter name, word or phrase works, it's best to stick with something that makes sense—big fat biker, for instance, may earn points for originality, but it'll probably just confuse your spectator. Unless, of course, said spec-

---

[2] Occasionally, due to a quirk in card placement, the chosen card will not yet have "migrated" to the middle of the pack by this step. If your spectator indicates that his card is still in an outside column, simply repeat the step one more time. Then you'll be set.

tator really is a big fat biker, in which case your trick will likely insult rather than confuse, in which case, you should wrap things up with a hasty disappearing act.

Next Easiest. First, tell your audience that you're going to turn over the cards one-by-one in order to find the chosen card. Then start peeling them off the deck and placing them face-up on the table. You know the correct card is the eleventh one, but keep peeling until you get to number thirteen (while, of course, noting number eleven as it's dealt). Then say, "The next card I turn over will be your card." The spectator will be feeling all patronizing and superior because, of course, his card is staring him in the face from the right there on the table.

"Stupid magician," he'll think. And you, being a wily conjurer, will take advantage of his confidence by offering to make a friendly wager on the outcome. He'll agree. You'll shake hands, and then, instead of turning over the incorrect fourteenth card that's next on the deck—as he'll most likely assume—you'll reach down and turn over Card eleven, the one that's already on the table. Flip it over and smile. Unless, of course, you're dealing with another big fat biker. In that case, my advice is to flip it over and run.

Most Difficult But Quite Astonishing If You Can Pull It Off. The "reveal" in this case is going to made to look like it's under the spectator's control. Fortunately, that's only the way it'll appear, since you will in fact be working the table like an evil puppet master, manipulating the cards at will. You've got to play this like butter, and you can only do it once. Any more than that, and your audience may catch on to your trickery. Here's how it works:

1) Start by placing the cards face down on the table in groups of two, one on top of the other in the shape of an X. With twenty-one cards, you'll be able to make ten piles; one card will be left over. Pay attention to the location of the eleventh card—for our purposes here, we'll call that the Star Pile. You must remember which pile is the Star Pile, and which of its two cards is the eleventh card.
2) Show the one remaining card to your spectator. "This isn't your card, is it?" you'll ask. He'll say no.

"Good," you'll reply. "Just checking." (Clever little script I've written here, is it not?) Toss the unwanted card aside with panache.

3) Have your spectator choose five out of the ten piles by pointing to them. If one of the piles he points to is the Star Pile, then quickly gather up and remove the other five. If he does not include the Star Pile among his picks, then remove each of the piles he chooses. It's important not to say anything beforehand like, "Tell me which piles to take away." Don't limit yourself to a certain action—whether you keep piles or remove them depends on whether or not the Star Pile is indicated.

4) You have five piles left, one of which is the Star Pile. Repeat the previous step, only ask your participant to choose three piles this time. Same process— either remove or retain depending on which piles he singles out.

5) You have two piles left. "Choose one pile," you'll say. If he points to the Star Pile, it stays; remove the remaining one. If he indicates the other pile, remove it. The two cards of the Star Pile will be the only ones left.

6) Have him chose one of the two cards remaining. Hopefully, you still remember which card—top or bottom—is the eleventh card. If he points to it, simply pick it up and show it to him: "Exactly!" you'll say. "This is indeed your card." If he points to the other card, then remove it from the table. The remaining card will be the one the spectator chose at the very beginning of the trick. Nice job, Houdini.

7) Act nonchalant as the audience hoots in applause. After all, this kind of thing happens all the time to great magicians.

By slyly making the spectator think he's controlling the exclusion of certain piles of cards, you're setting up a major payoff when the last card on the table—the one he seems to have picked at random—is the actual card he chose, but never revealed to you, way back at the start of the process. Again, you'll only be able to do this once. Otherwise you run the risk of the audience catching on

to the fact that sometimes you're eliminating the indicated piles and sometimes you're keeping them. Perform the trick with swift, smooth confidence, then move on to the next unsuspecting victim.

FINAL THOUGHTS

This is a great first-time card trick because it's so easy. There's no sleight-of-hand involved, no palming, no deck stacking, no trick cards. You can do it spur-of-the-moment—resting in the confidence that there's no chance the trick won't work when you deal and gather the cards correctly. In fact, you don't even have to have twenty-one cards. Any odd number will work, so long as you divide them into an odd number of rows and an odd number of columns (for instance: nine total cards separated into three columns of three cards apiece). After three dealings, the chosen card will always end up in the exact middle of your set.

In doing card tricks—or any type of magic—keep in mind that presentation is key. Even though your trick may be as simple as, in this case, knowing how to count, treat is as if you're operating amid a mind-blowing mystery. That means not telling anyone in advance what's going to happen. It also means refusing to explain how you did it once the trick's over. Do it once, flash a mischievous grin, and walk away.

Or, if you can pull it off, levitate away like David Blaine. That'll really impress them. Unfortunately, that's not something anyone expects you to know by now, so for any theories on self-levitation, you'll have to find another book. Sorry.

24 HOW TO COOK EGGS A BUNCH OF DIFFERENT WAYS

The year 1945 was a fine year to be an egg lover. You probably don't remember it, but those were good days for eggs. According to the American Egg Board (a Washington, D.C., group I didn't even know existed until I had to find some way to introduce this topic), 1945 was the peak year for egg consumption in the United States, as the average American consumed 405 eggs annually. That's more than an egg a day.

It's been downhill ever since, as tofu-snorting scientists and other cholesterol-obsessed spoilsports soon began demonizing the lowly egg as a bad food. Three decades ago, the American Heart Association urged moderation in egg consumption, believing an overindulgence of yolk to lead to clogging of the arteries and a host of other dietary problems. They recommended curbing egg intake to just three to four eggs a week. Humiliated chickens across the U.S. lowered their chicken coop doors to half-mast in sorrow. Egg-eaters followed suit. In 1997, the average American had reduced her diet to 240 eggs per year.[1]

But 1999 brought a dawn of good news: The AMA admitted it might have jumped the gun in devaluing eggs. That spring, a bunch of Harvard University researchers announced that having an egg a day is unlikely to increase the risk of stroke or heart disease in otherwise healthy people, unless, of course, those otherwise healthy people insist on cooking that daily egg in leftover bacon grease with a chaser of melted butter (which, admittedly, happens to be my favorite egg recipe, preferably cooked by my shivering father over a campfire in the thirty-degree chill of a summer morning in southwest Colorado's Uncompaghre wilderness).

---

[1] "The Good News About Eggs Just Got Better," *Egg Nutrition Center Online* Press Release, posted April 1999 (website: *www.enc-online.org/GoodNews.htm*).

Sigh. Before this devolves into a Proustian reverie, let's get back to the AMA—eggs, our nation's doctors have decided, are good for you when part of a healthy diet. Did you know that an egg contains nearly every nutrient known to be essential to humans? That an average-sized egg contains just more than seventy calories? That an egg is considered to be such an efficient source of protein that it is the standard by which the protein quality of other foods is measured?

Did you know that I'm accepting under-the-table cash from the American Egg Board for effusively shilling their product? Okay, okay, not really. But the point is this: Don't automatically write off eggs as nutritional nightmares. That social tendency is just the result of thirty years of bad press and bad plate associations, as eggs are generally eaten in combination with other foods that—to be completely honest—aren't so good for you. Bacon. Sausage. Toast slathered in butter. That's where you ought to be careful.

So the lesson here, friends, is that you should not be afraid of including an egg or two in your breakfast a couple of times per week. Which brings us to the following thing you should know: How to cook eggs a bunch of different ways.

Besides throwing around phrases like "Port du Salut makes a fine dessert cheese," an ideal way to let others know you're comfortable in the kitchen (or to make them *think* you're comfortable in the kitchen) is to display what's commonly known among the culinary elite as "Egg Skeellz." Not really. I just made that up. Still, there is no more impressive feat than a breakfast host, or brunch host, or midnight-on-New-Year's-Eve host asking, "How would you like your eggs?" and then cooking them to order. Here's how to do it.

FRIED EGGS

Start off with really fresh eggs, which will hold the best shape (shape being a main concern in frying a good egg, because everyone knows a lopsided egg don't taste as good as a lovely, concentrically yolked one).[2] Heat up a non-stick skillet. If you only have

---

[2] Grade AA eggs are the best for keeping their shape when you release them from their shells. They have a thicker albumen (the white stuff) and a firm yolk, and are therefore ideal for frying. If you ask an egg what he wants to be when he grows up, he'll say, "Grade AA." At which point you'll want to seek psychological attention because, let's face it, you're asking questions of your eggs and, even worse, getting answers.

a regular skillet, grease it with a small amount of margarine or cooking oil, remembering that this will likely add fat or calories. When the skillet is hot enough to sizzle a drop of water, it's ready. Break your eggs, one at a time, into the skillet. Some people prefer to break their eggs onto a saucer, then slip each egg off into the skillet from the saucer. To me, this is overly cautious and borderline anal-retentive. But to each his own.

Once the eggs hit the skillet, reduce heat to low. Cook the eggs slowly until the whites set and the yolk begins to thicken. For eggs sunny side up, stop here. (Keep in mind that eggs prepared this way often are not fully cooked.)

For eggs over-easy or, my favorite, over-medium, you'll have to cook the other side by gently flipping it with a non-stick spatula. Doing this without breaking the yolk can be the trickiest part of the process. It takes practice, dedication, and nerves of steel. And a really wide spatula, if you can find one. If you have trouble with the egg flip, you can cook the top side by spooning a little water or melted butter onto the egg, then covering with a lid. Just don't tell anyone you had to resort to the sissy method. Season as desired.

SCRAMBLED EGGS

Any fool can scramble an egg, right? Yeah, I guess so. But I've had scrambled eggs that were dry, rubbery, and barely edible. There are scrambled eggs and then there are good scrambled eggs. Here's how to make the latter:

First, break the eggs into a small bowl and use a fork or wire whisk to pre-blend the yolks and whites. Some choose to add a little milk at this point, for extra creamy eggs. Others may add a little water or melted butter. (According to my friend, Matt, water adds "fluffiness." Matt's weird, though.) Some recommend adding salt at this stage, while others insist this makes the eggs rubbery. I personally prefer to season my food when it's on my plate. Again, to each his own.

Preheat a non-stick skillet or saucepan at medium heat (or grease a regular skillet). Pour the egg mixture in, and then turn the heat down a little more. This is the secret to good scrambled eggs—low heat. If you allow the eggs to cook too fast or too much, you get the culinary equivalent of yellow packing peanuts. With a wooden fork, spoon, or rubber spatula, stir forwards and backwards all around the saucy eggs. Don't let the mixture sit long enough to get crispy on the edge of the skillet.

Don't don't don't turn the heat up. Just keep on stirring. Once most—but not all—of the egg moves from a creamy state to a solid, turn off the heat (the eggs should still be a little shiny and slightly underdone). Remove the skillet from the heat source, but keep scrambling until everything finishes cooking off the heat. Serve immediately. The mistake many people make is to stir the eggs over heat until done. Then they turn off the burner and the eggs continue to cook in the hot skillet. Silly people. Their eggs end up dry, overcooked, and chewy.

For kicks, melt cheese over your scrambled eggs. Or sprinkle on some chives. Or blanket them with a warm tortilla.

POACHED EGGS

Here's where you begin to enter the egg elite, as a well-poached egg is becoming a lost art. Start with fresh, refrigerator-cooled Grade AA eggs, which best allow the whites to gather neatly around the yolk.

Fill a medium-sized frying pan with a layer of water—two to three inches is ideal. Heat the pan to boiling, then reduce the heat as low as possible while keeping the water at a simmer. Expert's secret: Add a little vinegar and salt to the water at this point, which will help the eggs retain their shape. Break the eggs into a saucer, then dip the edge of the saucer into the water, sliding the eggs out to cook (you can probably pull off close to five eggs at a time, six if you're really heroic). Let 'em cook uncovered until the whites firm up. This usually takes between three and five minutes, depending on how solid you like your yolks.

Remove the eggs with a spatula or slotted spoon. Drain the eggs on a paper towel before serving. Try serving poached eggs on toast or a biscuit. For Eggs Benedict, combine them with an English muffin, ham or bacon, and hollandaise sauce.

OMELET

For a two- or three-egg omelet, start by hand-blending the eggs in a separate bowl with a tablespoon or so of water. Experts recommend using a fork for this, so as not to over-blend. Add a little grated cheese to the mix.

The most important next step is to use the right-sized pan. Six to eight inches is ideal. If your skillet is too large, it won't hold the heat as well, and a tough omelet will result. A small skillet makes the omelet hard to fold.

Swirl a tablespoon of butter over the surface of the pan until it stops foaming. Then, turn up the heat and pour in the egg mixture. Tilt the pan around so the eggs cover its entire surface. Leave it there five full seconds, then using a spatula, push the cooked mixture to the center. Tilt the pan and allow the uncooked part to flow back into its place at the bottom of the pan. Keep doing this until the omelet is slightly browned on the bottom and soft and moist in the center.

Add grated cheese and any other ingredients now by spooning them down the center of the omelet.[3] Tilt the pan again and, with the spatula, fold one-third of the omelet over the center filling. Holding a serving plate in the other hand, tip the omelet onto the plate; the final fold will occur as it rolls onto the plate. Remember, as with scrambled eggs, the egg will continue to "cook itself" due to its internal heat, so serve immediately.

HARD-COOKED (HARD-BOILED) EGGS

The easiest egg-cooking option. Place your eggs in a saucepan and cover with cold water (enough to cover the eggs by at least one inch). Bring the water rapidly to a boil, then cover the pan and remove from heat. Let stand for fifteen minutes or so. Then, cool the eggs down by first draining the hot water and then running cold water over them. Crack and eat. Decorate them for Easter.

---

[3] I recommend crispy bacon and mushrooms sautéed in Claude's® Barbecue Brisket Marinade Sauce. Claude's is a regional delicacy, though, so unless you live in Texas, you'll have to improvise. Or you can order it online at *www.claudessauces.com.*

Make egg salad. Juggle. The possibilities are endless.

A moderate serving of eggs is nutritious, delicious, and when cooked properly, quite impressive. If my dad can fry an egg over a campfire in frigid weather using a rusty pocketknife, some squeeze butter and a tiny Boy Scouts of America pan (circa 1964), then you can do it in the modern convenience and comfort of your home. So get crackin'.

25 HOW TO MAKE A KILLER FRUIT SMOOTHIE

The year was 1926. The world war was over. The stock market was booming. In London, something called "television" had been introduced when John Baird broadcast a doll on a tiny screen with flickering light. Plus, Milk Duds had just been invented. Things were good.

This was particularly true for a Californian named Julius Freed. In 1926, Freed opened a shop selling fresh orange juice in downtown Los Angeles, collecting a respectable twenty dollars a day from satisfied customers. He was more than content with the business, but his friend and real estate broker, an ex-chemist named Bill Hamlin, thought he could do better. As the story goes, Wild Bill got out his home chemistry set and compounded a frothy drink out of orange juice, milk, egg whites, and sugar. The mixture of the all-natural ingredients resulted in a juice-like liquid with a refreshing, creamy texture. Bill passed the recipe along to his friend, Julius, and they began selling the concoction at the juice shop. The response was amazing. Sales skyrocketed. The twenty dollars a day blossomed into one hundred dollars a day, and Mr. Freed's customers began to line up for the increasingly popular drink. Upon reaching the counter, they'd say, "Gimme an orange, Julius."

Bingo: product named. The rest is smoothie history. By 1929, Orange Julius stores had spread across the United States, and America had fallen in love with possibly the first and best-known fruit smoothie, a creamy orange drink with a cornball name.[1]

---

[1] Orange Julius franchise history located at *www.orangejulius.com/about/abo_history.asp*.

For unknown reasons (competition from astronaut-approved Tang™, perhaps?), the Orange Julius franchise began to fall from the public eye in the mid-80s, as did the humble smoothie culture it had spawned. Things looked bleak, until America kicked into a wellness mode during the nineties. Baby boomers reached middle-age, saw what was over the hill, and decided to get fit. The health club became a lifestyle, rather than just a sweaty room with mirrors. Vegetarianism became cool. Organic fruit became cooler. Consumers began drinking water from bottles, rather than the tap. A new fruit-whipping franchise called Jamba Juice started franchising in 1995. In 1997, Baskin-Robbins added the smoothie to its menu. And in 2002, Small Business Opportunities magazine labeled Smoothie King the number one franchise opportunity in the nation.

Dust off your blenders: The smoothie is back.

Despite the most obvious benefit of the fruit smoothie—by which I mean the deliciously calming way the word "smoothie" slides off your puckered lips (seriously ... say "smoothie" five times real fast, and darn it if you don't feel better about life in general)—it's also a hip, quick, tasty way to replenish your fast-food-slogged body. Smoothies are much more than a fun drink; they're good for you, too.

Here's why. According to the National Cancer Institute's "Eat Five a Day for Better Health" site (*www.5aday.gov*), only one out of four Americans eats the recommended serving of five fruits and vegetables on a daily basis. Yet eating a regular diet rich in fruits and vegetables can boost energy, fortify the immune system, and possibly even decrease the risk of cancer by nearly one-third. "An apple a day" is right.[2]

Best way to get those servings? The venerable smoothie. When made properly (that is, when made without four scoops of Cherry Garcia®, which, I'm sorry, does not qualify as fruit), smoothies are low in calories, low in fat, and high in vitamins, minerals, antioxidants, fiber, and overall cachet. Smoothies are the mixed drink of the new millennium.

---

[2] Centers for Disease Control and Prevention (CDC) 1998 Behavioral Risk Factor Surveillance Data.

A well-made smoothie has anywhere from two to four basic ingredients, depending on your taste. For the smoothie purist, there are two—and only two—building blocks to a good smoothie: fruit (one of which should be a banana) and juice. Drinkers with less refined palates often choose to add a thickening agent like yogurt, sorbet, or milk to the mix. And those who depend on the smoothie for a refreshing after-workout nectar like to blend in a few crushed ice cubes for texture.

Personally, I'm a fruit and juice guy, a purist. With the right ingredients, you can achieve a smooth, refreshing texture without the milk, ice, yogurt, or any non-fruit ingredients that can add extra calories and carbs to your drink (not that there's anything wrong with that). What are those ingredients? Simple: A banana (any degree of ripeness will do), frozen fruit (buy it in a bag at any grocery store), and juice (choose your poison, but make sure it's 100 percent juice, and not, for instance, Grape Nehi).

And you need a good blender.

MAIN INGREDIENTS

Bananas. Because they provide natural sweetness to counter the tartness of most fruits, bananas are key to a good smoothie. For general eating purposes, I like my bananas slightly green and lose interest once they start spotting brown. When that occurs, I put the browning bananas in the fridge. This stops the ripening process (at the cooler temperature, they'll still turn brown on the outside—really dark, nasty brown—but keep their firmness and taste), and these refrigerated bananas become smoothies within a day or two. It doesn't hurt that they're already cold when their time comes. (Just don't let anyone see you drop that discolored banana into the blender. And don't forget to peel it first.)

Fruit. Use your imagination. If you're mixing in a banana, almost any other fruit will form a flavorsome complement. Again, the idea is to use frozen fruit. Most general-interest fruit is available in your grocer's freezer—peaches, strawberries, blueberries, raspberries. Smoothie aficionados pay particular attention to bags of mixed fruit. Try a berry blend, which contains a combination of the three berries listed above and is an excellent source of fiber. Also available in many places is a melon blend, which packages honeydew, cantaloupe, peaches, and blueberries together. Feel free to pop any fresh fruit you have into the freezer for an hour or two before use. Using already frozen fruit keeps you from having to feed ice into the mixture (which can be difficult on the blender and may water down your drink). The fruit cools down the smoothie and gives you a softer, consistently slushy texture. (Note: Don't let the frozen fruit rule keep you from also adding whatever fresh fruit you have on hand. Kiwis make great smoothie ingredients, as do fresh nectarines, pineapples, mangoes, and pretty much anything else.)

Juice. Most smoothie recipes call for orange juice, but again, feel free to experiment. Many companies are now offering several varieties of mixed juices (strawberry-grape, orange-pineapple-banana) that work nicely for smoothies. If you're using frozen fruit, then cold, liquid juice is fine—simply add it to the blender along with the fruit. If the fruit is fresh, not frozen, it's a good idea to use frozen juice concentrate—the kind of juice that comes in the little cylindrical containers (don't forget to add water to dilute the concentrate). This will give you a nice, slushy base. And who doesn't love a nice, slushy base?

ALTERNATE INGREDIENTS

Some people like to give their smoothies a little extra zip in addition to fruit and juice. If made properly, these alternate ingredients aren't necessary for proper texture or taste—the right combination of frozen fruit and bananas should handle that—but they can turn a regular smoothie into a smoothie with kick. They'll also add calories, so keep that in mind. Here are a few of the favorites:

Yogurt. For a thick, smooth consistency, consider adding a half-cup of nonfat yogurt. Plain or vanilla is a good choice for providing a nice balance to the fruit, but you can also get great results from flavored versions. Yogurt is an excellent source of protein, riboflavin, and vitamin B-12, and is considered a better source of calcium than a glass of milk. It helps strengthen the immune system by adding healthy bacterial cultures to your stomach. (Try not to use the phrase "bacterial cultures" while serving your smoothie, though. Some things are better left unsaid.)

Milk. The old stand-by for making stuff creamier. Adding milk is a good way to load a smoothie up with protein and calcium. Using reduced fat (2 percent) or skim milk is the best bet for keeping the fat grams and calories of your smoothie at a reasonable level.

Sorbet. A frozen desert with high fruit content, sorbets make excellent smoothie ingredients. As a plus, they're dairy-free, so a sorbet smoothie will be safe for the lactose intolerant or those who can't use milk or dairy products. Sorbets come in a variety of fruit flavors and are the secret ingredients to some of the most savory smoothies. Sherbet is pretty much the same thing as sorbet, taste-wise, but it contains milk.

RECIPES

Following are a handful of easy recipes for smoothie-making. Try them out. Reward yourself. Impress your friends. Use that blender your aunt gave you for graduation. Enjoy the fruity goodness. Just remember that smoothie recipes are just suggestions. Like rules, they're made to be broken.[3]

Banana-Berry
20 oz. orange juice
1 banana, peeled (duh)
1 cup frozen strawberries
Blend and serve. Makes two large servings.

Breakfast Blend
1 banana, peeled
12 oz. pineapple juice
½ cup low-fat vanilla yogurt
1 cup frozen strawberries
Blend and serve. Makes about two small servings.

Berry Peachy
20 oz. orange juice
1 banana
½ cup fresh peaches

---

[3] Except for the important rules, like not harming your fellow man or taking his property. And stuff like stop signs. And the one about waiting an hour before swimming after you eat. Don't break those rules.

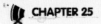

1 cup frozen mixed berries (strawberries, raspberries,
blueberries)
Blend and serve. Makes two large servings.

Green Giant
3 kiwi fruit, peeled and sliced
Half a banana
1 cup skim milk
1 tbsp. fresh lemon juice
1 large scoop lime sorbet
Blend the kiwi, banana, milk and juice about ten seconds, then add the sorbet and mix on low until smooth. Makes a couple of servings.

Cantaberry Tale
20 oz. cranberry-grape juice
1 banana
1 cup frozen strawberries
1 cup fresh cantaloupe, diced
Blend and serve. Makes two large servings.

The year is 1980, and Thomas Payne is just plain tired of being alive. Born in the waning years of the 1800s, Payne is older than the century he lives in and barely able to get up each morning. He's dying of heart disease. Twenty-four hours a day he fights shortness of breath and debilitating chest pain, choking down multiple cardiac medications to keep his heart from folding in on itself. Life has gotten hard, so Tom Payne decides to end it.

His solution is a unique one. Whether he's just more creative than the next guy or physically unable to find the strength to do it right, Payne settles on an unconventional means of self-destruction: He decides to run—literally run—his ticker into the ground. On a crisp spring morning, he opens his back door, bounds down the steps, and tears through the yard into the alley behind his house. At a dead run (snicker, pun intended) he traverses the alley and stumbles into the street. He makes it about a hundred yards before collapsing into an octogenarian heap at the edge of the curb. "This is it," he wheezes, and then everything turns black.

But he's wrong. That isn't it. A few minutes later, Payne regains consciousness and, with severe disappointment, comes to the conclusion he isn't dead. He vows to try again the next day, and for good measure, flushes his heart medications down the drain. Prevention is irrelevant to the suicidal.

Morning number two. Payne takes a deep breath, bursts through the back door, down the steps, across the yard, past the alley and into the street. Gasping for breath, his legs and chest burning, he lurches a few steps past the previous day's point of collapse, then passes out again.

Morning number three. (Our man Mr. Payne is nothing if not determined.) He tries to kill himself again, same method. Gets a little further. You see where this is going?

For several days in a row, he erupts through the back door, hoping each run will be his last. Every day, he gets a little farther before losing consciousness. Then finally, one day, he doesn't pass out at all. Nothing and everything happens at once. He keeps running and running and running. And a smile creeps upon his face.

Before long, Tom Payne is jogging a slow-paced six miles a day, still unmedicated, and still alive. He makes it a hobby. Eventually he works his way up to marathons, and within a few years, becomes a cult figure on the fitness and jogging circuit—the old man at the finish line, tanned and trim. The geezer's attempts at suicide ended up healing him.[1]

There are a couple of valuable lessons to be learned from the true story of Tom Payne. First, attempting to jog oneself to death is one of the worst suicide strategies I've ever encountered. I'm no expert, but I can think of a dozen or so more efficient methods right off the top of my head. Payne was tenacious, but certainly not the smartest sock in the drawer. Besides—there's so much to live for, it's not worth it, your life touches so many others' lives, George Bailey, etc.

Second—and most important to our discussion here—is something I'm sure you realize already: Exercise is good for you. Daily exercise is not just a defensive strategy to keep your arms from flabbing and your gut from sagging, nor is it simply a means for weight control. No, its virtues run much deeper—regular exercise can benefit you as much as eating a balanced diet or getting a regular checkup at the doctor. It reduces the risk of heart disease by improving blood circulation throughout the body. It lowers cholesterol levels, manages high blood pressure, and prevents bone loss. Exercise boosts your energy and helps control stress. It releases tension. It improves your self-image, results in a better

---

[1] Payne's story first appeared in an old edition of the *American Medical Joggers Association Newsletter* (date unknown) and is recounted again by Alan Clark, M.D., in the article "A Is for Aerobics" on the St. John's Health System (Springfield, Missouri) website: *www.stjohns.com/medinfo*.

night's sleep, and helps fight anxiety and depression. Point being: We all should exercise a bit more.

The snag is that, for many of us, a lifestyle of fitness seems inaccessible due to time, money, or physical constraints. Why? Because the act of staying in shape has gotten wrapped up with the health club culture. We associate "getting exercise" with going to the gym, wearing fancy workout clothes, strapping into a space-age weight-training machine, or signing up for classes full of sexy, 1-percent-body-fat, pneumatically gifted Energizer® bunnies. In such environments, the intimidation level runs nearly as high as the bunnies' energy levels—and nothing will knock the legs out from under an exercise routine like the mistaken belief that you need to look like Jennifer Aniston to be considered healthy.

For many people, then, mistakenly equating a gym membership with exercise makes fitness seem nearly impossible. Not everyone's cut out for it, including me. I'm scrawny and pale, and had trouble just bench-pressing the weight-lifting bar—the forty-pound bar, mind you, with exactly zero weights added to it—during my brief P.E.-class foray into weight-training when I was fourteen. I was a ninety-pound weakling. Still am.

The good news is that you don't have to sign up for expensive gym memberships to stay in shape. You can do it all by yourself, with no expensive equipment, no embarrassing clothing, and no glistening hardbodies nearby to mock your tonelessness. Here's something you should know by now: Keeping fit is much easier than you think. All it takes is the creativity and determination of Tom Payne. Without all the suicidal tendencies, of course.

GYMS ARE FOR SISSIES

Okay, that's not extensively true. Some of my best friends are members of gyms or health clubs or fitness centers or whatever you want to call them. They attend religiously and fit in workouts and aerobics classes on a daily basis. They've found fitness clubs to be very beneficial, from providing access to equipment and programs they don't have at home to boosting productivity through social motivation (getting to the end of a Cardio-Funk session in a class of twenty is loads easier than completing it by yourself at home). And I hear that the gym is a great place to meet people, though I entertain a suspicion that a certain body type is required for this to be true. For example, I don't imagine any gorgeously fit young female saying, "Check out the pasty dude in the corner—the one trying to bench-press the bar. He's hot. You think he needs a spotter?" (To which the obvious reply would be, "Pasty dude? Where? Behind that climbing rope?")

But every time I drive by the local exercise studio on the way home from work, I wonder something about the shimmering bodies chugging away on the treadmills and cycles: Did they drive their cars to the gym?

How many people do you know who will drive two miles to the health club, at which point they climb onto the treadmill for a two-mile jog? Or hoist themselves onto the exercise bike for several minutes of non-destination pedaling? Maybe I'm missing something. Maybe there's something to be said for watching *Everybody Loves Raymond* while riding a bike or striding upon an eternal slab of rubber, but wouldn't it be just as beneficial to actually walk or run to the gym, where you could then participate in some other health-related activity? Or to cut out the expensive membership altogether and just go out and exercise in the real world?[2]

For me, half of the joy of jogging is experiencing the fresh morning air. It's about breezing past well-maintained yards before the sun comes up, about watching the wild cottontail rabbits zig-zag across the nearby park when they see me coming. It's about the off-chance someone's sprinkler system will switch on while I'm in its spray zone. It's about finally making it back to my driveway and catching my breath at the moment the sun crests the horizon. Jogging outdoors is an adventure.

Jogging on a treadmill is, well, monotonous as a hamster wheel. Same goes for cycling. And don't get me started on the folks who ride the elevator at work, then go to the gym for a stint on the stair-stepper at the end of the day.

---

[2] And by "real world," I'm referring to your neighborhood. Though some would argue that the well-manicured, over watered lawns surrounding the fake Tudor homes of American suburbia—furnished with "authentic" Pottery Barn replications of eighteenth century apothecary tables—aren't exactly paragons of reality. But anyway...

Here's the point: We are surrounded by opportunities to stay fit throughout the day, but because we're conditioned to associate exercise with the health club, we're blind to them. Something tells me we're due for a redefinition of "exercise."

MOVE, BABY, MOVE

Exercising at the gym requires three things—time, money, and sexy fitness apparel (which is generally tight on the top and loose on the bottom, involves some percentage of Lycra®, and costs a pretty penny). One or all of these can be a hindrance to your average twentysomething. Some of us don't have the time to commit to a daily or weekly gym routine—I'm happy some days just to carve out time to relax, which, to me, doesn't include working out. Others don't have the cash to join a club, which can begin at a basic thirty or forty bucks a month and grow from there. And still others don't look good in Lycra®. You know who you are.

Or rather, I know who I am.

All of these things can add up, becoming prohibitive to people who'd like to exercise but just can't make the commitment. Fortunately for you, there's a simple solution to this problem. It's time to reconsider our definition of exercise.

When most people think of exercise, they probably picture one of the following activities: weight-lifting; a bouncy, cardio-intensive group workout like kickboxing or cardio-funk; recreational sports like basketball or volleyball; or a formal regimen of solo activity such as jogging, walking, or biking.

We can do better than that by making exercise less formal. Instead of confining it to the examples above, let's identify exercise by one all-important attribute: movement. Exercise employs some form of movement toward the task of maintaining fitness. It means pumping your legs and flailing your arms, and doing so at a pace that gets your heart beating a little faster. Work in some good arm and leg movement on a daily basis, and you've got yourself a gym-free, weight-free, Lycra®-free lifestyle of fitness.

Consider housework. The simple activity of operating a vacuum cleaner requires movement. It involves work; that's why we call it

a chore. Next weekend, how about burning calories and boosting your heart rate by vacuuming with vigor? Put a little drive into your dusting. Scrub the tub with enthusiasm. Mow the yard, pull weeds, dig up the flower bed with gusto—gardening can burn as many calories as some health club activities. By adding a little energy and extra movement to your Saturday routine, you can turn a necessary, mundane task into an opportunity for exercise.

Sound too easy? Maybe so, but that's the beauty of the movement plan—it eases fitness into your busy lifestyle by locating it in unexpected places. One of the best ways to put it to work requires undergoing a simple reversal of mindset, which is to ...

REJECT CONVENIENCE

Ours is a culture that wants convenience, and wants it now. Or sooner, if you can swing that. We expect express lanes at the supermarket, express oil changes at the quick lube, and express credit card processing online. We clamor for drive-up pharmacies, drive-up coffee shops, drive-up dry cleaners, and—here's a shot of pure-grain irony for you—drive-up liquor stores (which, remarkably enough, are still permitted in twenty-three states, one of those being my home state of Texas). We'll spend ten minutes circling a parking lot in order to find a more convenient parking space, never realizing that, had we parked as far away from the store as possible at the beginning and simply started walking, we'd be inside by now.

O-ho! Therein lies example one in the case for movement: Every time we opt for convenience, we pass up a chance to exercise. The next time you go to work or school or the mall, pay attention to the way you do things. Make every decision as you normally would, but be aware of the missed opportunities. Do you take the elevator to your fourth-floor office instead of using the stairs? Do you make a phone call or dash off an e-mail to a co-worker when you could just as easily walk down the hall and talk in person? Do you ride the escalator from one floor to the next at the mall, staring past the hardy souls shlepping their shopping bags up the adjoining staircase? Do you contentedly watch children running and playing at the park, or do you actually run and play with them? Have you ever considered walking to the video store, rather than driving? Or—heresy!—deliberately misplacing your television remote control, forcing yourself to get off your arse to change channels?

Now, remember, I didn't say staying in shape was easy. But it is simpler than you'd think. Rebelling against a life of ease is one way to exploit the many chances for fitness we encounter every day. But if you absolutely have to use your remote control, or ride the elevator, you might consider another option, which is to ...

GET OUT AND WALK

You know how Mom used to always say, "It's so nice outside. Why don't you kids go out and play?" It wasn't just because you were annoying her by piling up couch cushions and pillows and blankets and doing flips onto them as part of your plan to become a circus acrobat (although, in retrospect, that might have played a tiny role in it, at least in my family). Mom was trying to do you a favor—research indicates that going outside is good for you. In a recent survey conducted by RT Neilson for Recreational Equipment, Inc. (REI), the popular specialty outdoors retail chain, more than 70 percent of Americans said that outdoor leisure activities are more effective in relieving stress than indoor ones. Nine out of ten respondents indicated that spending time outside lifted their spirits.[3]

So do you have to mountain bike, snowshoe, or kayak to exercise outdoors? Nope. Although those activities do carry something of a cool quotient, they can be just as expensive as a gym membership. A more reasonable idea is to just go outside and walk. According to the National Institute of Health and the Dietary Guidelines Advisory Committee, thirty minutes of light activity every day is enough exercise for the average person.[4] Why not make that thirty minutes of outdoor walking?

Perhaps you think you're too busy to find that kind of time, but let me be the first to tell you this: You're wrong. Because according to my secret plan, you can do it at work. Most working Joes take a couple of fifteen-minute breaks during the day, one in the

---

[3] "Small Tracts," *Common Ground: Conservation News from the Conservation Fund* (January-March issue, 2002), 4.

[4] Regina Halsey, "Government's New Advice: Exercise Every Day," CNN.com (Posted January 2, 1996, at *www.cnn.com/HEALTH/9601/dietary_guidelines*).

morning and one in the afternoon. Add that to a half-hour or hour-long lunch break, and you've got plenty of time during the workday to get moving. Instead of hanging out by the coffee machine or browsing eBay during your breaks, why not get some fresh air? Walk around the block a few times. Explore the neighborhood around your office. At lunch, pick a restaurant ten minutes from the office and walk there and back. Keep a steady pace. If the weather gets bad, walk up and down the halls or climb staircases.

Fitting physical activities into your daily routine will do wonders for your lifestyle. It'll refresh your spirits, burn calories, and increase your energy level. You'll look better, feel better, and perform better simply by making your body work a little harder during the day. Be aware of how lazy you've become—how lazy we've all become—then do something about it. Change your habits, defy convenience, thumb your nose at our too-efficient society.

There's nothing wrong with going to the gym, of course. If you can afford the time and the expense, then by all means, make it a part of your day. Good for you. But for those of us who can't, we have to find our own way to stay in shape. Luckily, these opportunities are right there in front of us. They've been there the whole time, like the backyard and alley and streets behind Tom Payne's house. All we need is a reason to start, and the motivation to get back up after we stumble and pass out.

Just make sure your motivation isn't the same as Tom's. That would be bad.

27

HOW NOT TO WORRY

For some reason, I have lots of early memories of my childhood—early, as in two years old and under. I'm not sure why. Perhaps it was a genetic slip of fate, a neurological hiccup that kicked my long-term memory into gear before it ought to have been driving, so to speak. Some have speculated that it's a blessing from God. I disagree for a simple reason: Most of my early memories are bad ones.

I was a shy, cautious, worried child, probably because I carried around with me the following scenes from my childhood.

Memory No. 1: Blood. It's bedtime, and Dad and I are reading a Heckle & Jeckyl comic book. In it, the two bickering black crows are in a department store on an escalator. Suddenly, I feel a tickle in my nose, and onto the white bed sheet appears a soaking splotch of red. My first nosebleed. The blood freaks me out, and I have ever since associated those cartoon birds with a vague feeling of dread. I'm not bothered at all by blood these days, but the memory remains unsettling.

Memory No. 2: Disneyland. I'm eighteen months old, according to my mom's records of a family trip to California. At the park, we go on some sort of submarine ride, and being relatively new to the concept of theme parks and attractions in general, I accepted the ride as the real thing. In fact, until I revisited the Magic Kingdom as a nine-year-old, my erroneous memory was of being in an actual submarine descending into the ocean. Through the windows of the submerged ship, I recall peering into the water (a six-foot-deep concrete pond, painted blue on the sides and bottom) and seeing tropical fish (fake), undulating underwater ferns (plastic) and mermaids (phony as your uncle's toupee). Then we passed a couple of sharks, and I panicked. My immediate conclusion was that the sharks were going to eat the mermaids. Again—freaked me out. Fear kicked in, my bladder failed, and I started screaming as only a toddler can do. Mom was embarrassed; the ride ended shortly thereafter. I was haunted by this recollection of scenes until things were cleared up during that second trip to Disneyland. Still, not a pleasant memory.

Memory #3: The Sesame Street pie man. Back in the mid-1970s, as *Sesame Street* was hitting its stride, there was an oft-repeated sketch of a Muppet baker descending a flight of stairs with a tray full of pies. Details are hazy, but the pie man would always stumble on the stairs and drop the entire tray. Pies flew. As you might expect by now, I couldn't deal the pie man's failure very well. According to my mother, she would have to monitor my *Sesame Street* viewing, and warn me when the sketch came up. (Sigh) I would hide behind the couch until it was over. Seriously. The visuals remain vague because I probably only watched the sequence once or twice. But I can tell you exactly what the back of the couch looked like. And I can almost taste the apprehension.[1] Issues, much?

I introduce this topic with these "poor, sad, deranged Jason" anecdotes to make a point: Everyone experiences anxiety in some form or fashion, and at every age. Preschoolers, adolescents, adults, the elderly—we all deal with worry. It's a natural part of life (though, in all honestly, normal children shouldn't be driven behind the couch by a program as harmless as *Sesame Street*). But get off my back—the 1970s were difficult for a lot of us. Just ask Danny Bonaduce.

As a child, I could create my own anxiety simply by recalling

---

[1] Strangely enough, my daughter, who will turn three in April of 2003, has a similar reaction to a current *Sesame Street* sketch in which Big Bird injures his ankle while playing basketball. When she viewed it the first time, she was just slightly concerned, but it made an impression. She talked about it many times over the next few days, telling her grandparents and preschool teachers that Big Bird hurt his foot—at that point, she was very matter-of-fact about it. But eventually she ruminated over the scene so much it "tipped," turning into a full-fledged source of anxiety to her. Now, if Big Bird is shown playing basketball *at all* (whether it's the actual offending scene or not), Ellie goes into a panic, and we have to turn the show off. So either I'm not as messed up as I thought ... or I've passed on my problems to my kids. Hmmm.

these miniature traumas. Even today, the associated visuals, sounds, and smells they bring are perfectly real. And as a child, the anxiety attached to these memories was just as tangible. Just thinking of Heckle & Jeckyl was enough to stir up an indistinct shadow at the corner of my consciousness. The shark-and-submarine memories conveyed a powerless fear. And don't get me started on the pie man. Life as a four or five year old should be care-free, but I negated it on occasion by dredging up bad memories.

And that's when simple feelings of apprehension, anxiety, or fear slide from natural impulses into unnatural stumbling blocks—when they threaten our basic happiness. Worrying is one of those impulses, and it brings us to something you should know by now: Needless worry knocks years off your life, so we should try to keep it to a minimum. Easier said than done, right? Afraid so. Let's look at some specifics.

WHAT IS WORRY?

In scientific terms, worry is closely aligned with our "fight or flight" instinct. When faced with a potentially dangerous situation, humans have an immediate emergency impulse to either: 1) defend ourselves or 2) scream like a girl and run away in trouser-soiling horror. Problem is, we humans aren't real good at the first option, ninjas and vampire slayers aside. We're slow and energy-inefficient. Our teeth aren't especially pointy, our nails aren't particularly sharp, and we're not able to confuse predators by expelling foul clouds of ink like an octopus.

Which is too bad, really.

So we try a different "fight or flight" tactic—control. Over the centuries, this impulse has manifested itself physically in the form of weaponry. We learned to forge steel and harness gunpowder in order to control dangerous animals and other humans. Mentally, we exert control another way. It's called worry.

In some situations, worry is good for us. Psychologists recognize that people become more efficient and productive upon encountering situational anxiety. It's what drives us to roll up our sleeves and finish a project on a tight deadline. It allows us to keep a level head during a medical emergency. Situational anxiety is something all humans experience and is completely natural. It's fueled by adrenaline, lasts for a brief period of time, and occurs proportionately to the circumstance.

But there's also a bad kind of worry, and it can be a problem. It occurs separately from any external pressure or circumstance. It's driven by insecurity rather than external forces. It's destructive instead of helpful and tends to blow things out of proportion. While situational anxiety wears off with the circumstance, destructive anxiety is persistent. It grabs you by the brain and refuses to budge. Soon, it'll begin to break you down physically, leaving sleepless nights, headaches, ulcers, depression, or even a suppressed immune system in its wake. Not good.

Let's put it in real-life terms. It's late at night, you're asleep in bed, and suddenly you're startled awake by the noise of glass breaking. Without a hint of grogginess, you sit up immediately. Your heart's racing, your palms begin to sweat and your breathing becomes shallow and slightly labored. That's good—the "fight or flight" response has kicked in. Should you find yourself experiencing the same physical sensations upon, for instance, discovering a coffee stain on your pants on your way to work (unfortunately, not your typical "fight or flight" situation) then the anxiety has gone too far. Read on.

WHY DO WE WORRY?

For most of us, the destructive kind of worry goes like this. Something occurs that causes us to feel like we're losing control— for instance, we're burdened by an overwhelming project at work. As the responsibilities stack up, and our sense of control diminishes, we feebly attempt to regain it by asking, "What if?" *What if I can't get everything done on time? What if that makes the company lose money? What if they blame it on me? What if I get fired? What if I can't pay my bills, and the bank defaults on my loans, and they repossess my house, and I can't find anywhere to live, and I find myself deranged and homeless on the streets of Manhattan, smoking used cigarette butts stained with lipstick and telling people to call me "Captain Whitestockings" when I beg them for change? And who will take care of my cats?* Worry is our way of preparing ourselves to face the unknown by focusing on the worst-case scenario. It's like personal damage control—by expecting a terrible outcome, we feel honest relief when things don't turn out as bad as we thought.

The problem is that the end result—the relief—is not proportionate to the process. In the hypothetical case above, being pleasantly surprised when you buckle down and finish the project on time is hardly worth the sleepless days prior to that, during which you imagined yourself wearing Hefty bags and digging through the trash behind Jack-in-the-Box. Nor does it cancel out the ulcers you developed along the way, or the viral infection you caught due to your weakened immune system—a sickness that'll doubtless lead to other worry. *What if I start vomiting and can't stop? What if I get dehydrated? Is this what kidney failure feels like? Where'd those spots come from?* And so on.

HOW CAN I STOP WORRYING?

It's hard, because many people are chronic worriers, permanently existing somewhere on the anxiety scale between general pessimism and incapacitating fear. Simply telling them to stop worrying is like telling someone to stop digesting food.

There's a chance these extreme worriers suffer from a medical condition called Generalized Anxiety Disorder (GAD), which is said to strike more than four million Americans every year.[2] It's a chronic condition, characterized by six months or more of exaggerated stress at a level much more severe than what's considered normal. GAD sufferers worry about money, health, family, or work, even when those areas of life are trouble-free. They live in a constant state of concern, expecting the worse, teetering on the edge of depression. They may even entertain suicidal thoughts. If you fall into this category, the following suggestions probably won't help much. Talk to your physician about it, and describe how you feel and any symptoms that accompany your worry (aches and pains, insomnia, fatigue). The answer might be professional care, cognitive therapy or medication—or some combination of the three.

---

[2] Statistics from National Institute of Mental Health website: "Facts About Generalized Anxiety Disorder" (*www.nimh.nih.gov/anxiety/gadfacts.cfm*), updated June 28, 2002.

If your worry is less severe, here are a few steps you can take to regain control:

1) Check your medicine cabinet. Some prescription medicines and over-the counter products like nasal sprays, diet pills, and decongestants can sometimes generate feelings of anxiety.

2) Cut back on the caffeine. Because it stimulates your nervous system, too much caffeine may also increase nervousness. Go figure.

3) Exercise regularly. When stress levels rise and you feel like there's just not enough time in the day to get things done, one of the first victims is regular exercise. Bad move. Exercising regularly not only keeps you physically healthy, it pumps up your mental well-being, too. You feel better about yourself. And that, in turn, combats anxiety.

4) Learn how to relax. Activities like prayer, deep breathing, listening to soothing music, or doing yoga all are powerful stress-breakers. Find some way to take your mind off the worry and relax, even if it's something as simple as counting backwards from one hundred.

5) Give worry a time and place. Some mental health experts actually recommend chronic worriers allow themselves a controlled, self-regulated anxiety session once a day—but on their terms. Designate a specific time and place to worry about stuff. When that time comes, spend thirty minutes or so thinking about your worries and what you should do about them. Make a checklist or devise a plan of action. Don't focus on what might happen, but on what you can do to take care of it. Then return to your day. If any other worries crop up, sweep them into the corner until your next "worry session." Stick to your schedule and you'll begin to regain control.

The most important thing to remember when anxiety starts to creep up on you is to take some form of action. When the piles on your desk grow to high-rise level, find a way to work more efficiently or delegate. Do medical research online if you're confronted by a family sickness. Take charge of your finances when money gets tight. Do something—anything—to help you exert some control over your anxiety. Just sitting around thinking too much, marinating in worry, is the worst thing you can do.

Feelings of anxiety and the "what ifs" they engender can be scary, but for the most part, they're meaningless. Many of our worries are concerned with the past—mistakes we've made, pain we've experienced, foibles, and failures—but you can't change the past, and why worry about something you can't change?

Many of our worries concern the future, but I'd be willing to bet 95 percent of these negative "what ifs" never happen, and the worrying is probably worse for us than the anticipated danger itself. Besides, the future hasn't been written yet—it can change. Why waste energy on unlikely outcomes? Take action instead. Take control.

And will someone please let me know before the pie man comes on television?

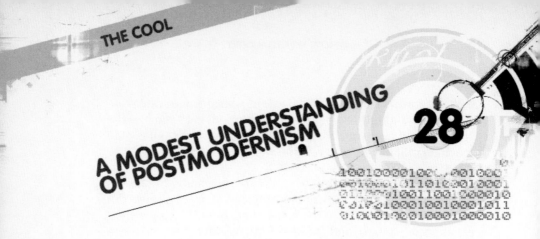

A MODEST UNDERSTANDING OF POSTMODERNISM

28

Q: What do you get when you cross postmodernism with a mafia don?
A: Someone who'll make you an offer you can't ... understand.

The above joke and its variants are making their rounds on philosophical online message boards, and it pretty much illustrates what we're all thinking: What the devil is postmodernism? You've undoubtedly heard of it. As a concept, it gets bandied about every acre of the college campus, from lectures on architecture to theological debates to, especially, the philosophy and literature halls. But that's not the only place. "Postmodernism" the idea and "postmodern" the adjective show up as often in discussions on pop culture as the tragedy that is Michael Jackson's face. In fact, the two have a lot in common: They're everywhere, they're incomprehensible, and both can be downright scary.

From *Newsweek* to *New Republic*, *Slate* to *Salon*, the millennial media are increasingly defining contemporary culture by the term "postmodern." It's used to explain almost everything—the music of Beck, the films of M. Night Shyamalan, the fiction of Don DeLillo, and television programs from *The Sopranos* to *The Simpsons* to *Survivor*. The rush to play the postmodern card has become so prevalent I get the feeling that postmodernism is to pop culture aficionados what *Finnegan's Wake* is to the literary elite—something everyone talks about but hardly understands.

"Pomo" (as the cool kids like to call it) is the buzzword of our generation, and everyone seems to have a different idea of what it means. It's been identified as both the downfall of traditional religion and the savior of the church. It's derided for the rise of P. Diddy and praised as the creative energy behind *Seinfeld*. For some, it's our generation's bridge toward optimism, hope, and community. For others, it's the next stop on the train to nihilism. And, to think, it all started with a bunch of well-meaning architects. Let's begin there, making it our springboard toward a working understanding of what postmodernism is. For one thing, it's something you should know by now—or at least something you should be able to identify on occasion.

WHERE IT CAME FROM

This is the hard part, so let's get it out of the way first. Recognizing postmodernism is fairly easy and even fun. Trying to explain it is not. It involves all sorts of philosophical underpinnings and revolutionary stances against big ideas like "reality" or "truth." It requires a basic familiarity with the theories of Lyotard and Derrida and of Nietzsche before those. It calls for awareness of literary criticism (deconstruction) and of conceptual sociology (marginalization). But most of us have already started to doze off by now, and furthermore—what was I saying?

Let's get on with it. You'll need some background, so here it is: Postmodernism started as an architectural movement, the central concept of which was a dismissal of the doctrines of the "modernists"—those architects who, up until the 1950s and 1960s, were the cat's meow because they were all about skyscrapers and ambition and "the new," whatever that means. They latched onto the "go where no man has gone before" *Star Trek* perspective because, by golly, they were intelligent and rational scientific beings and could do almost anything. They liked parallel lines and right angles, glass and steel and chrome. Examples of modern architecture? The Sears Tower in Chicago. The Guggenheim, and all of Frank Lloyd Wright's work. And, of course, the twin towers of the World Trade Center.

Postmodern architecture took a deep breath and, rejecting the modernists' cult of individuality, tried to combine the practicality of the modern with the beauty and comfort of the classic forms of the past. It wanted the best of both worlds, so it merged them via architectural "collage." A classic example of postmodern architecture can be found in the wave of baseball stadium-building during the nineties, wherein futuristic domes and cold, cavernous, symmetrical stadiums were bulldozed and replaced by comfortable, asymmetrical, technologically advanced facilities—brand-new facilities that retained the quaint look and cozy feel of old-time ballparks. Baltimore's Camden Yards is a prime example.

Postmodernism eventually slid from architecture into philosophy and the arts, and from there into everything else. Modernism—which began way back during the Enlightenment—was centered around Man as the sole source of reason and truth. In response, postmodernism rolled its eyes and said, "whatever." It denied the idea of the sovereign individual and, instead, emphasized diversity, collective experience, the malleability of truth and the dissolution of distinctions.

Goodbye, John Wayne. Hello, *The Matrix*. Let the confusion begin.

WHAT IT IS NOW

As you might expect, as postmodernism crept into the culture at large, it began to take on a few wonky characteristics, which can be expected when one of your core values is "the dissolution of distinctions." Or, to put that phrase into a simpler, more polarizing package: relativism.

These characteristics take various forms, some of which remain very complex. But perhaps its most important contribution to our culture is its questioning of reality: Pomo has a fundamental distrust of what philosophers call "metanarratives," those theories that help us explain how the world works. What is a metanarrative? Christianity is one. Evolution is another. Science, history, Marxism, Religious Determinism—each of these big "stories" defines our environment based on a set of absolute values and concrete ideas. Postmodernism is skeptical of these big stories, though, because a grand, all-encompassing theory neglects the originality and influence of the little stories. But here's the dilemma: The big stories form the basis of what we consider truth, and when they are untrustworthy, then our only recourse is to treat any idea of absolute truth with skepticism.

The main byproduct, then, is an emphasis on multiple truths rather than one all-encompassing one (remember, the focus of postmodernism is on the collective, not the individual). Therefore postmodernists live in a lot of uncertainty. They always question: Are the ideals of developed countries better than those of the third-world, or is it just that we have more opportunities for advancement? How can I believe so strongly in the monotheistic Judeo-Christian God when people all over the world believe just as strongly in hundreds of other gods? Can I truly say democracy is the answer to nation-building when I see so many flaws in the U.S. system? Is Carrot Top really that annoying or am I just conditioned by my Western education to think so?

Postmodernists have lost faith in human knowledge and systems. As a result, we don't have a whole lot to cling to anymore—not religion, not mankind, not even reality (which, in the pomo way of thinking, is a creation of the surrounding culture, and may or may not be "true"). This foundation-less condition is often referred to as the "postmodern void." We're all kind of just floating around, picking up little scraps of philosophy and shavings of religion and bits of culture but not knowing whether to trust them or not.

Postmodernism is fun, huh?

WHAT IT LOOKS LIKE

I'm a visual learner, so I find it easier to understand postmodernism via real-life examples rather than by reading a tedious explanation of it. So let's pan away from theory and adjust our focus: What does postmodernism look like at street level? What are its characteristics? What kinds of shoes does it wear?

As expected, our starting and ending point is popular culture. Some examples of postmodernism in action:

TELEVISION: 'FRIENDS'

In modern sitcoms like *Laverne & Shirley* or *Everybody Loves Raymond*, humor is derived from the situations in which the characters find themselves (like trying to out-bowl high-school nemesis Rosie Greenbaum or wondering how Ray's parents backed a car into the living room). The stories are simple and straightforward; they take place in our modern society, where things go wrong and hilarity ensues.

In *Friends*, a postmodern show, the humor derives from two sources: the situations and the shared history (collective experience) of its audience. For instance, one episode cast plaintive singer Chris Isaak as a regular guy. We then hear his character sing with an idiosyncratic Chris Isaak-like falsetto, which is immediately followed by Lisa Kudrow's mockery of his singing style (Phoebe to Isaak: "You might want to find a more masculine note"). The joke depends on our familiarity with both Isaak and his music.

TELEVISION: 'SEINFELD'

Without a doubt, *Seinfeld* was television's boundary-busting postmodern poster child. On a weekly basis, the lines between real-life and fiction were not only blurred, they were erased so hard the paper tore. Consider: Jerry Seinfeld, the comedian, played a comedian named Jerry Seinfeld. At one point in this show about nothing, George and Jerry developed a sitcom about nothing for a fictional NBC, based upon their TV lives on the real NBC. Then they cast look-alikes of their characters. This is the kind of thing that gave Aristotle ulcers.

That's not all. The postmodern principle of shared history was given considerable emphasis in almost every episode. Characters discoursed on actual elements of our culture, from Melrose Place to Junior Mints. At the height of our nation's O.J. obsession, Kramer hired Jackie Chiles, a fast-talking sleaze ball lawyer patterned after Johnnie Cochran (Chiles even went so far as to rhyme in court). The employment of the famous Zapruder film in Oliver Stone's *JFK* was parodied with a grainy reenactment of Keith Hernandez (a real-life ballplayer, formerly of the Mets) spitting "one magic loogie" on Kramer and Newman.

As opposed to modern sitcoms, in which the audience is assumed to know only what occurs within the context of the show, postmodern programs like *Seinfeld* take it a step further: The characters exist in the same world we do, and the humor depends on our bringing an awareness of that world to our viewing experience.

Other postmodern television shows (some current, some not): *Ally McBeal, Buffy the Vampire Slayer, Curb Your Enthusiasm,*

Mystery Science Theater 3000, Scrubs, The Simpsons, The Sopranos, South Park, The X-Files.

FILM: 'THE MATRIX'

A major premise of the postmodern worldview (recognizing the fact that, technically, such thing as an overarching worldview—a metanarrative—isn't really allowed by pomo) is that reality is subjective. It's flexible. How it's perceived is based on how we've constructed it, through our language, environment, upbringing, even our economic status. Postmodernism says we see the world we've accustomed ourselves to seeing, but what we're seeing isn't necessarily real. (For instance, Hindus, fundamentalist Christians, and atheists all look at the world with different eyes, filtering every event through unique lenses. Each group believes to have the "correct" viewpoint, based upon its religious metanarrative or lack thereof. They can't all be right, can they? Can they all be wrong?)

These are the kinds of questions alluded to in the sci-fi thriller *The Matrix*, which pretty much explains that reality—the world we eat, sleep, work, and love in—is a big lie.[1] Turns out computers took over the world several years back, made us slaves, and put us in a perpetual dream-like virtual reality state. Keanu Reeves embodies Neo, a computer geek who stumbles upon the deception, learns to manipulate the constructed reality (the "Matrix"), and finds himself a messianic leader of the underground rebellion.

The Matrix takes a gloomy view of the world but was immensely popular upon its release in theaters (and found an even greater audience on DVD, that most postmodern of media[2]). Its central

---

[1] I know *The Matrix* isn't exactly the most recent postmodern film, but since everyone's seen it and its over-hyped mythology has become embedded in our culture, I deemed it a prime example.

[2] As long as we're categorizing, a movie on video would be considered modern. It's linear, straightforward and mechanical. A DVD, on the other hand, is decidedly postmodern. You can watch the movie itself, or a version of the movie playing beneath the director's audio commentary. You can view it from the beginning, or scene-by-scene, or in another language. Often, you can watch a behind-the-scenes documentary of the film during production, which literally deconstructs the sets and images as shown in the theater. The reality of the film—that which premiered at the cineplex—is shattered, reassembled and then expanded by DVD. That's postmodern, baby.

message—the need to question what can be seen—is sticky: It stays with you after the credits roll. Upon leaving the cinema after viewing it the first time, blinking into the bright sunlight, I thought how nice it was to walk out into the normal, peaceful world of 1999. Then I realized that the deceived characters in the movie probably thought the same thing. And they were wrong ... way wrong. What if I was wrong, too? That kind of skepticism is twenty-four-karat postmodernism.

Other postmodern films: *A.I.: Artificial Intelligence, Adaptation, Being John Malkovich, Blade Runner, Blue Velvet, Monty Python and the Holy Grail, Scream, The Sixth Sense, The Truman Show.*

MUSIC: MOBY

One of the first big-name stars of techno/dance music, Moby— along with genre-defying contemporaries like Beck and Radiohead—epitomizes postmodernity as it applies to music. A vegan militant Christian punk environmentalist non-drinker non-smoker non-druggie rave DJ descendant of Herman Melville, Moby is a lot of different things, many of them contradictory. As his popularity has grown, his philosophical lyrics and soft-spoken interviews have indicated a discomfort with consumerism—particularly as it applies to the music industry. Yet his ambient 1999 album, *Play*, famously licensed each song for advertising. Hmm.

In his music, the distinctions between musical genres are arbitrary. Listeners to a typical song are likely to hear a hip-hop drum beat laid over a textured tapestry of sampled sounds, which might include a female voice trilling a gospel ad-lib, the riff of a jazz trumpet, a grunt or two from James Brown, and a twinkling snippet of classical piano thrown in for good measure—this in addition to Moby's own lyrics and a main vocal. Eclectic doesn't begin to describe it.

Most of the tracks on *Play* and his 2002 release, *18*, sample other forms of music—particularly early twentieth century gospel and blues recordings—then blend those forms into a separate, contemporary mix. Like building a car from junkyard parts, Moby takes pieces of old music and assembles them into a sonic collage you can groove to. This "borrowing" and recontextualizing of history is classic postmodernism.[3] Other postmodern musicians or bands: Beck, John Cage, Chemical Brothers, Eminem, Fatboy Slim, P. Diddy, Pavement, Radiohead, Regurgitator, Smashing Pumpkins, Frank Zappa.

THE INTERNET

Our fascination with postmodernism as it applies to all aspects of culture—and not just architecture and literary theory, where it began—has grown side-by-side with the all-encompassing symbol of our times: the Internet. And the Internet, itself, is profoundly postmodern.

While linear narrative (that is, top-to-bottom telling of a story) exists in many forms on the Web, it is challenged by Web users' tendencies to surf via hypertext. For example, someone might begin reading an article about dogs until they get to the name of a breed they've never heard of, perhaps the Finnish Spitz. The name is highlighted via hyperlink, so the reader jumps to a completely separate site to read up on the breed. The reader might eventually return to the original article, but is just as likely to end up somewhere else, reading something unrelated. Thus is the non-linear nature of the Internet; the direction-less fluidity that's one of its major selling points is also a distinctly postmodern characteristic.

So is the nature of reality online, where you can be whatever (or whomever) you want to be. Users in chat rooms and message boards discourse in anonymity, known only by names like "LovePuppy43" or simple avatars. Identity is elastic. Websites are easy to assemble and upload, and therefore much of the information online is not to be trusted. It leads to a number of vital questions about the online experience: What is real? What is accurate? What can I trust? How did I end up at this porn site when all I wanted was to sell my David Lee Roth bobblehead on eBay?

Because it's hard to define, because it challenges our understand-

---

[3] Recontextualizing: A pretentious ten-dollar word, but it works for describing the process of taking something out of one framework and putting it to use in another—in Moby's case, wrapping a contemporary dance track around a line of 1920s Mississippi Delta blues.

ing of truth, and because it seems to include everything and nothing at once, postmodernism can be scary. Pomo is fragmented and sloppy. It's snarky and ironic. Rather than ignoring the past, it respects it, but is just as likely to take that history out of context and put it to some unexpected use. Postmodernism values community. It emphasizes diversity and plurality. It says all ideas have value, all ideas are worthy of discussion—it just won't let you go around saying they're absolutely true.

And that's why lots of people don't like it. While it may be all-inclusive, it can also be a major challenge to any tightly-held belief, from Christianity to science to capitalism. The trouble is, being uncomfortable with the idea of postmodernism is much like a fish being distressed by living in water: Sorry, fish, but there's not much you can do about it. We are a postmodern generation because the world we live in is a postmodern one.

You may not like it, but postmodernism is here to stay; that's why you need to understand it. And now, thanks to this chapter, you do. Probably. At least, I hope so. Okay, maybe not, but at least you've heard of it. That's a good start.

EPILOGUE

THERE'S MORE TO LIFE THAN ROMANCE, MONEY, AND POKER

Three stories.

One: Motivational guru Zig Ziglar tells of a memorable revival service led by early twentieth-century evangelical firebrand Mordecai Ham, who is perhaps best known for being the preacher on the night of Billy Graham's conversion. One evening, before taking the podium to deliver his typically fire-and-brimstone sermon, Ham was approached by a stranger. The man pulled the preacher aside and said, "Mr. Ham, I'm here because I'm curious. But I just want you to know that I don't believe in heaven, I don't believe in hell, I don't believe in God, and I certainly don't believe in prayer."

Ham thanked him for his honesty and stepped onto the stage. He addressed the large crowd. "Folks, we've got an unusual man at our service tonight. He doesn't believe in heaven, doesn't believe in hell, doesn't believe in God, and certainly doesn't believe in prayer. So I want all of us, the entire time I'm preaching, to pray that God will kill this man before I'm through."

As soon as the words left Ham's mouth, the non-believer leapt violently from his seat and elbowed his way past his fellow congregants into the aisle. He sprinted toward the door and burst out of the building, all the while screaming at the top of his lungs, "No! No! Don't you do it! Don't pray that! Please, don't you do it!"[1]

Everyone believes in something.

Two: In the early nineties, when I was in high school, my grandfa-

---

[1] Zig Ziglar, *Success for Dummies* (Foster City, CA: IDG Books Worldwide, 1998), 190.

ther Brownie (you might remember him as the grocery shopping expert from chapter seventeen) was diagnosed with laryngeal cancer. A malignant tumor was discovered on his voice box. Due to the strength of the disease, only one real solution was offered—a total laryngectomy. So they took his voice away.

After having the larynx removed, patients can learn to speak again by pursuing a couple of options. The first is to use a mechanical or artificial larynx, a device held up to the permanent hole in the neck (called a stoma) that remains following the operation. The device converts air vibrations into sound. You can understand someone who speaks with a mechanical larynx, but they sound like an inflectionless robot.

Option two involved learning to talk in a completely new way, via esophageal speech. It's accomplished by gulping air into the top of the esophagus and then forcing it back out—speech by way of a glorified burp. The burp vibrates the walls of the throat, producing sound that's shaped into words as it travels through the mouth. Esophageal speech is difficult to master and the resulting sound is low-pitched and gruff. But you can inflect it, and it's all your own.

Brownie tried the mechanical larynx for a few days but hated it. So he chose door number two and went to work. After a grueling year, he'd taught himself to talk again. And to sing. And even to laugh.

You need to know this about my grandfather: He's the very definition of a tough old coot.[2] My memories of Brownie before his cancer surgery are of a hard-working, secretly kind but outwardly stern retiree, one whose demeanor befitted an ex-Marine military policeman, which he was. But after the surgery, during the process of learning to speak, the most surprising thing happened—over the course of the most difficult year of his life, Brownie's outward disposition did a 180.

---

[2] For instance, at the age of seventy, Brownie was mowing his lawn when he accidentally fell over a six-foot retaining wall. He landed headfirst on the top of his shoulder and blasted his rotator cuff to pieces. So what did he do? He finished mowing. Then he went inside and carried on with his business. Several days later, he finally went to the doctor because he couldn't lift his arm over his head to get dressed. It wasn't that big of a deal, he told us at the time—just inconvenient.

I first recognized it one evening playing Ping-Pong with him.[3] He slammed the ball at me, it bounced off my chest, I made a face, and Brownie laughed. Not a regular laugh, but an esophageal one—an exaggerated wheeze. Not content with the primal release of the wheeze-laugh, Brownie switched to a physical one. He doubled over at the waist and started slapping his knee, his face lit with a denture-rich grin. Then he slapped the table, wagged his head, slapped the knee one more time, wheezed again, and finally straightened back up.

Brownie had just executed a full-body laugh. And from that point on, he became the most enjoyable laugher I've ever been around. I honestly don't remember him expressing much amusement before the surgery; I'm certain he didn't laugh near as much then as he does now. Brownie's life is a lot funnier these days, and when something tickles him, you know it. The raspy laugh hisses out from deep inside him, like a burst of air from a leaky tire; then the knee-slapping kicks in. His internal joy wells up into an external burst of movement, and it's wonderful to see. It never fails to make me grin.

Three: In 1946, Dr. Percy Spencer, a self-taught engineer with the Raytheon Corporation, was testing a new vacuum tube called a magnetron during a radar-related research project. During the test, he felt a strange sensation, and reaching into the pocket nearest the magnetron, he discovered that the candy bar he'd placed there had completely melted. This intrigued him, so he did an experiment. He held a bag of unpopped popcorn kernels near the tube. They popped.

Another test the next day: Spencer and a curious colleague placed an egg next to the magnetron tube. They watched as the egg began to shiver and wobble, a result of pressure against the shell caused by the egg's rapidly rising internal temperature. Suddenly the egg exploded, spraying hot yolk onto their faces.

Spencer, widely regarded as an electronics genius, figured out what was happening. The energy of the low-density radio waves emitted by the magnetron were agitating the water molecules in

---

[3] He used to defeat me regularly when I was in high school. Now, at eighty, the guy still beats me four out of five times, and I'm a pretty decent table tennis player.

the food products, making them vibrate and spin. The molecular gyrations caused friction. The friction generated heat. As opposed to a range oven—which cooks food slowly from the outside—Spencer had discovered a way to heat things up internally, and to do it much faster. He soon harnessed those magnetron waves into something usable, then gave his invention a name: the "radar range." Today we call it the microwave oven.[4]

We all believe in something. And like a knee-slapping wheeze laugh or an explosion of yolk, that interior belief will eventually make its way to the surface. The inside can't stay inside for long, and the quality of that heat makes us who we are. Such is the case for religion—or as it's known in our dogmaphobic society: spirituality.

Here in the technology-driven infancy of the twenty-first century, the quest for the spiritual has reached a weird juncture. Church attendance has held steady over the last few years, as 43 percent of American adults attends a church or religious service during a typical week. Yet, according to the Barna Research Group, more than one out of every five adults under the age of thirty-five consider themselves to be agnostic, atheistic, or affiliated with a non-Christian faith—a percentage that's more than two times higher than that of our parents' generation.[5]

Those numbers tell us a couple of things. First of all, we can assume that young adults don't necessarily equate "spiritual" with "Christian." While generations of Americans before us operated within a strictly Christian worldview, that's not so today. Christianity is only one of many viable faiths to our informed, open-minded society, and is being treated as such.

Second, young adults are exhibiting a growing interest in spirituality, but are looking for it outside the typical church structure. Smack in the middle of a suffocatingly materialistic culture, we're still on a quest for meaning and purpose—but that search is now much more expansive. We're exploring new faiths and challeng-

---

[4] Don Murray, "Percy Spencer and His Itch to Know," *Reader's Digest*, August 1958, 114.
[5] "American Faith is Diverse, as Shown Among Five Faith-Based Segments," Barna Research Online (posted January 9, 2002, at *www.barna.org/cgi-bin/PagePressRelease.asp?PressReleaseID=105&Reference=B*).

ing old ones. The reason for this is obvious: The old guard has failed to satisfy.

It's at this point that I should reveal that, yes, I am a member of the old guard. I am a Christian. I am a believer. What do I believe in? Plenty. I believe the sun's going to come up in the morning. I believe the chair I'm sitting in will support me until I stand. I believe in the power of my body to keep itself going—heart beating, liver functioning, lungs breathing for at least another fifty years or so—and that I'll awaken from my next sleep. I believe in the authenticity of my daughter's hugs, and that the flash in my newborn son's eyes is the light of recognition. He knows me.

I believe in God. He knows me, too.

At times it can be a difficult belief, one that doesn't come as easily to me as it did when I was younger. It's challenged on a daily basis by the injustice of our fellow humans and the ridiculousness of the religious, by the prevalence of unmitigated evil and uninhibited disaster. Ten years ago, my faith was the simple assurance that the Judeo-Christian Jehovah, as revealed in the person of Christ, was and is absolutely real. Today, on a good day, I still hold to that. But on a bad day? On a bad day, faith for me is living as if God's real, but ... wondering.

Mine is a limping, bandaged version of Christianity, one that is more likely to wince at the weirdness of my faith than embrace it. I cringe at the Falwells and Robertsons. I groan at the Left Behinds. I'm not amused by American Christianity's rising irrelevance, its gradual movement to the fringes of culture while, nevertheless, attempting to appropriate the music and entertainment and marketing strategies and political tactics of that very culture for its own use. I'm no fan of the way we try to impose man's structures on God, because I seriously doubt He's just a glorified, holy version of the white republican male. I'm tired of the bullheaded dogmatism of the evangelical church and its increasingly misguided priorities[6]—but despite the baggage, the Christian church is a foundational part of my life.

---

[6] Like focusing too intently on political issues like school prayer, social issues like homosexuality, or eschatological issues like the second coming—at the expense of immediate needs like hunger and poverty.

It's flawed and ugly and, often, just plain wrong. The thing is, so am I.

That's why the church remains my home. It's where I live.

So my wobbly faith remains in place, hanging at times by a thread, but still, somehow, attached. My faith is something I hope to model for my kids, just like my parents and grandparents before me. It is the common ground that connects me to my closest friends. It's the tingle I get when standing thigh-deep in southwest Colorado's Cebolla Creek, surrounded by God's playground of Aspen and silence and wary trout. It's the invisible backbone to the earlier chapters on generosity and selflessness and optimism and even romance.

It's what gives my life meaning—and that's what most of our human pursuits ultimately come down to: the search for meaning, the reach for significance, the hunt for wisdom. Why? Because I firmly believe there's more to Jason Boyett than blood and flesh and bone and nerves and gray matter. I have to think that we're not just here to procreate and survive and get bigger and better and stronger as a race, that there's more to life than staying alive as long as possible. That things like joy and grief and contentment are more than just chemical reactions and firing synapses— though, undoubtedly, biology has something to do with it—but that they are connected to *something* greater. A "deeper magic," as C.S. Lewis called it in *The Lion, the Witch and the Wardrobe*.

I have to believe we each have a soul. And if we have a soul, then another question follows, this one more difficult: What for? An easier question to answer is the converse: If there's no such thing as the soul, then what the hell are we living for? If it all ends in nothingness, then what's the point?

Which brings us to the title of this chapter. We've dedicated a bunch of pages to discussion of things we ought to be aware of at this juncture in life. Some have been marginally serious, others practical, a few downright silly. But none are the end-all of existence. Making wise financial decisions won't guarantee a fulfilling life—there are too many rich people funding psychiatrists to support that theory. Love, sex, and dating? They can make you feel warm and fuzzy—but warm and fuzzy are poor combatants against hardship. Poker? Groceries? A decent resume? Not a chance.

The thing that gets us through life is hope. Hope that we're right about the soul thing. Hope that life's tiny coincidences and pockets of emotion are evidence of something greater. Hope that the light at the end of the tunnel isn't an oncoming train.

Hope that this confusion we feel—this confusion I feel about who's behind the curtain, about the nature of coincidence and the glory of fly-fishing and the light in my kids' eyes—that these are, in themselves, the evidence of God. And, to paraphrase St. Augustine of Hippo, "Why worry about understanding? If you think you understand it, it's not God."[7]

The questions, the lack of understanding, the uncertainty, the search for God—these are what make us human. They are the microwaves that get our molecules to spinning. They agitate us. They cause internal friction. The process is not always comfortable, but it does lead to change, and change is good. The eventual release of internal pressure, like hot yolk bursting through a cracked shell, is a soothing act of destruction. It makes things feel right again.

That's why, despite the discomfort, I keep putting myself as close to the microwaves as I can. That's where the heat is. That's where the soul begins. That's faith.

And that faith led me headlong into the person of Jesus Christ, whom we Christians believe to be the incarnation of God: Jehovah dressed in a suit of His own creation. I don't get what Jesus says a lot of the time—and I'm not alone, based on the number of Christian denominations in the world, each claiming a different understanding of the Scriptures—but I generally like it. I like the anti-establishment parables He told, the way He got the angriest with the pious religious people and showed kindness to the drunks and prostitutes and lepers. I like the way He chose a dozen uneducated, incapable commoners and occasional nitwits to become His disciples.[8] I like the way He seemed to treat children

---

[7] St. Augustine of Hippo, *Sermons* (Sermon 117,5: PL 38,673).
[8] Which, to my mind, is akin to President Bush asking Carrot Top to serve as one of his closest advisors.

and women as equals in a male-dominated world, and how His social teachings were always wrapped around selflessness and humility and giving and unconditional love—relational ideas that were so unusual at that time and in that place. And I like the way He offered grace and forgiveness and mercy with no strings attached.

I like that most of all.

When my grandfather lost his larynx, he lost the mechanism to do the stuff that once came so naturally. Singing. Speaking. Laughing. Disease stripped them away, and all that remained was an empty throat. The stirring was still there—he still had the words inside him, he still had the capacity for joy—but the mechanism for releasing them was gone. He had to relearn those things. He had to remake his voice and his laugh and his song with the damaged scraps he had left.

Now his raspy voice is even sweeter. Brownie's laughing is not only more frequent, but more enjoyable, because it's a fight his whole body commits to in a flurry of wheezing, knee-slapping, waist-bending fury. Each laugh is a battle, but when it finally gets to the surface, it's good.

Brownie's story is also the Christian one: a natural Eden spoiled by the disease of sin; the emptiness of the sin waging a violent conflict with the longing of the soul; the deeper magic struggling toward the light. In Christ, we find the new mechanism for release. We find a new way to talk, to laugh, to sing. It often requires more of us than we'd like to give—in a fallen world, life is harder than it was intended to be, more complicated than necessary—but the end result is a spiritual body laugh.

And achieving that laugh? That is what we're after.

All of us believe in something; all of us need a little religion. And a lot of religions have much to offer the world. The postmodern, all-inclusive thing to do would be to say they're all virtually the same, just multiple paths to a single destination. That may be true—like I said, for every one rock-solid answer I have about my faith, I have a dozen other squishy questions—but I'm not ready to concede that yet.

EPILOGUE

Because from where I am, the burden of Christian faith—in all its frustrating, misunderstood, *Left Behind*-reading glory—seems to make the most sense. It gives me hope. It offers meaning. It stirs my soul. It heats me up, wheezes from me in a guttural laugh, and occasionally bursts from my shell in a blast of yolk.

It's important, at least to me, so I thought you should know about it. That's all.

ALSO FROM
JASON BOYETT...

IT'S NOT JUST ABOUT SPENDING LESS. IT'S ABOUT LIVING MORE.

Cheap Ways To... won't only give you insider tips on how to save a few bucks in almost every part of everyday life, it will also help you find ways to get more out of what you already have.

Available now.
Check your local bookseller, or visit RELEVANTstore.com